T0380936

Joy in the Journey

Experiencing God on the Appalachian Trail

Sue Hatch

WestBow Press books may be ordered through booksellers or by contacting:

WestBow Press
A Division of Thomas Nelson & Zondervan
1663 Liberty Drive
Bloomington, IN 47403
www.westbowpress.com
1 (866) 928-1240

Scripture taken from the New King James Version. Copyright 1979, 1980, 1982 by Thomas Nelson, inc. Used by permission. All rights reserved.

ISBN: 978-1-9736-7807-6 (sc)
ISBN: 978-1-9736-7808-3 (e)

Library of Congress Control Number: 2019916866

Print information available on the last page.

WestBow Press rev. date: 01/17/2020

WestBow
PRESS®
A DIVISION OF THOMAS NELSON
& ZONDERVAN

DEDICATION

This book is dedicated to Marilyn Hatch who inspired in me a love for adventure and to the myriad of believers whose footsteps have left imprint on my spiritual journey. You know who you are.

TABLE OF CONTENTS

VIRGINIA

VIRGINIA

Grayson Highlands
6-14-06

Dave's Place,
Damascus, VA 6-13-06

Kincora Hostel, Hampton, TN
6-10-06 + 6-20-06

Miss Janet's, Erwin, TN
6-3-06

North

Standing Bear Farm,
Hartford, TN
5-26-06

Fontana Dam, NC
5-22-06

Happy Talk
GA-VA
'06
Phil 4:8, 9

Hiawassee, GA
5-13-06

Springer Mountain, GA
5-7-06

GEORGIA

JOY IN THE JOURNEY: EXPERIENCING GOD ON THE APPALACHIAN TRAIL

INTRODUCTION

Is it possible that we are not entirely on our own as we travel life's journey? When we're feeling weak or tired, don't we just call the doctor, open the refrigerator, or take a nap? What do we do when we're thirsty? Don't we just get a drink and not give it another thought? Yet, God said to ask, "Give us, this day, our daily bread," (Matthew 6:11 New King James Version), and we are promised a life of joy as he abides with us.

People in biblical times knew what it was to rely on God when they were weak or thirsty, and the Bible is full of references to God's provision, sufficient for every need. Moses and the Israelites were in the wilderness forty years. They were traveling on foot and carrying whatever they needed, relying on God. The Apostle Paul walked all over the Mediterranean as a missionary. He was a tent-maker, relying on God. Could they even imagine the comforts of my culture? Could I imagine a life of such dependence? Whose was the greater blessing? I had claimed a relationship with God since the age of twenty-three, yet I did not know this God.

I believed that God is alive and well and involved in my life. I sought to test that belief through a fast — not a fast from food, rather a fast from distractions in order to focus on God. Forty days on the Appalachian Trail (AT) seemed the perfect place.

Joy in the Journey is about living in dependence on God and the joy of finding him faithful. "These things I have spoken to you, that my joy may remain in you, and that your joy may be full." (John 15:11 King James Version)

PART I THE PRE-HIKE

The Appalachian Trail is said to range from eighteen inches wide to the width of a major highway. Actually, there are times it is only as wide as a boot print. Most of the time, it is a navigable path marked by white blazes painted on rocks or trees.

In just five million steps, a person can walk from Springer Mountain in Georgia, progress through thirteen other states, and reach Mount Katahdin in Maine, only 2,175 miles away, give or take a few as improvements are made.

After doing a little research and obtaining some gear, I set out in October 2005 on a pre- hike, starting at Amicalola Falls, Georgia, on the 8.8 mile Approach Trail. Going north I would reach Springer Mountain, the southern terminus of the Appalachian Trail. Some adventurous souls, known as thru-hikers, would hike the whole 2,175 miles in four to six months. On this pre-hike, I would spend two or three nights in the woods. The trail was noted to be difficult in this section and I thought it would be an ideal place to start, to determine if I was even capable of living in the mountains with nothing but a pack. If I followed the chalkboard eraser-sized blue painted blazes marking the trail to Springer, I would then continue a few miles to experience following the white blazes that mark the Appalachian Trail and then retrace my steps to my car at Amicalola.

The following are passages from the journal I kept to record my first northbound section hike of the AT. If I succeeded then I would continue preparing for a May 2006 start on what I hoped to be a forty-day hike, which if I averaged about ten miles a day might bring me to Virginia. Lord willing.

THE APPROACH TRAIL

Monday, October 10, 2005

Great day. 57° at noon. Overcast. Misty to drip from the trees but no rain. Left Amicalola State Park at 12:30 PM headed toward Springer Mountain on the Appalachian Approach Trail wearing a little less than thirty pounds on my back, (forgot to weigh after I'd added a few extras). Blue blazes to follow. Saw a bear at 2:30 and a little sunshine right after. Decided it's a good sign if a black bear crosses your path...better than one coming down the path toward you. He was way more scared than me--that is, he was running head first down the side of the mountain, in total disregard for switch backs and signs that read, "Remain on marked trail," whereas I stayed calmly on the path, plodding along, adhering to all the rules. I heard that you shouldn't look a bear in the eye, who would? So I pretended not to watch him fall down the mountain, or see if he had any friends still on the other side of me. Just kept plodding along with huge ears.

There were campsites with fire pits every thirty minutes or so along the trail, which was encouraging because I was pretty sure I didn't want to stay at a shelter. I came through a place where the trail was all overgrown with some sort of flowering bushes and a flock of towhees twittering about. It was neat to go through and hear the fluttering of their wings. I flushed a couple of large birds which I heard but never saw. Heard and saw a big woodpecker, Redheaded? I think so. He marked a rhythm for me for a long while, well, sort of, just get the bug and get back to something I can walk or sing to!

The sign said the trail from Amicalola to Springer was strenuous. I'd also read in the books that hikers say it's one of the toughest sections. Very steep. I had to focus on getting over that next rock, another root, one more rock, etc. I had to watch each step. One of the thru-hikers I read about told how many steps it took to get from Georgia to Maine. I know he didn't really count, but I could identify. There was a place where the path was broad and level and I almost fell. Interesting. Complacency. On the narrow path you're focused. Sermon on the Mount.

Stopped at 5 pm at a site beside the trail. A trail maintenance guy stopped by but I saw no other man nor beast. Set up the tent and fixed couscous which I had packaged with some extras in individual plastic bags. My little alcohol Pepsi-can stove worked perfectly and I heated enough water to pour into the couscous bag, from which I ate with some hot chocolate. Licked my spoon and cup clean to put away. Put my cocoa trash in my empty couscous bag and clean up was done. Went to bed at 6 with yummy in my tummy. Gentle breeze, dripping trees. Solitude. Peace.

Tuesday, October 11, 2005

I got up at 7:20. Good rest last night. Woke several times to check my watch. My tent is an MSR Hubba, single person-sized. Small person, one who doesn't roll over, sit up or play dead. Well, play dead would work. Sometime during the night I had to relieve myself. I had already decided I would not go outdoors to tend to that business and had devised an excellent plan: go in a plastic bag and dump it out the door. Don't try it. It doesn't work. You can't hold the bag right and the urge doesn't wait. Fortunately I thought of that so I had moved my sleeping bag to one end and stood my mat up along the side. While I was cleaning up the floor I heard this grunting noise outside at the head of the tent. Oh great! A wild pig was grubbing around and I thought, "He smelled what I just dumped and now wants to eat me!" I didn't breathe and had my eyes wide open...so I could hear better in the dark...? He stopped. I waited until I just had to breathe again, still nothing, so resumed my cleaning and repositioning my mat. There it was again! My mat rubbing the side of the tent. So much for wild pigs eating me.

Breakfast of bacon bits which I ate quickly and quietly so no bears would be attracted to the sound of the plastic wrapper or the pungent odor of the bacon, and oatmeal with raisins and wheat bran, all eaten from a plastic bag, and a Folger's coffee single, tea-bag fashion. I discovered my pot had a leak so I had to cook sideways. Back on the trail at 9. Passed the water spot on Black Mountain at 9:50. Decided to wait and get water at Black Gap. Guide book says I can see Springer Mountain from here. I think I see it but not that sure of where I am or what it looks like.

10:00 am. 57°. Overcast but the sun peeks. Butterflies accompany me along the trail.

I heard low flying helicopters. Some hikers told about Army Rangers in the area. They "stormed" a shelter and scared the people half to death. They said heads popped out from everywhere. What some people do for entertainment. It made me work a little harder finding a place for relief along the trail. Is that a bush or a camouflaged army guy I'm squatting behind?

11:05 am. Arrived at Black Gap Shelter. Saw the cables for hanging food bags. They were designed so that a bag could be hoisted by pulleys out of the reach of bears. Looks like they'd work. This was actually safer for bears as well as humans because a bear that has lost its fear of humans could become tagged as a nuisance bear and could be destroyed.

I knew about hanging food, but the cables were at shelters and I preferred to sleep in the woods. I came prepared. I had a nylon knee-high and a string. That first night I put a rock in the nylon and threw at a limb for all I was worth. After getting bopped in the head several times, I decided to forget the whole thing and commit the cardinal sin: sleep with my pack. That's right. My bag was packed and prepared in a way that I would not smell like food as I walked along. The food was in so many layers of nonporous bags that I thought it could not possibly attract even an ant. And so I hiked.

I planned to get water there but somebody wrote in the shelter register, "Can't find water anywhere!" and that hiker backtracked to the water I'd just left. Oh great. I dug out my trail guide and followed the directions: across the trail and down the hill. L-o-n-g, steep hill. Found a nice stream. Waiting for water treatment to finish now. Didn't prepare well for this. I had twenty-ounce Coke bottles. So how many drops? Had to use a quart zip lock bag to collect and treat the water, then add it to the bottles after twenty minutes. Drank or wasted what I couldn't put in the bottles. Gave me time to catch up on my journal. While in the shelter I made my first register entry and signed with my self-appointed trail name: "Happy Talk," from Rogers and Hammerstein's *South Pacific*.

Trail names were fun. The proper thing to do might be to wait for the name to be assigned by fellow hikers but many chose their own and I had my reasons for choosing "Happy Talk." Some people were only known by their trail name and usually used it to sign the register.

A guy at the Falls said my name left a lot to live up to. Hadn't really thought of that, chose it more for the song, about having a dream to make a dream come true. Actually, I'm glad I didn't make it to Black Gap Shelter that first night because a lady hiker had put in the register how her pack was ruining her trip. She would not have wanted to hear about my excellent pack. Happy talk can get a little sickening, I suppose. Anyhow, he's right. No talk of bad stuff. This is about me and God and hope and the future.

FIRST AT SECTION-HIKE: SPRINGER MT TO LONG CREEK FALLS

Tuesday, October 11, 2005

Made it to Springer Mountain at noon. 8.8 miles from Amicalola. Elevation: 3,782 feet. Clear sky. Great view. The blazes have changed from blue to white, officially marking the Appalachian Trail which I have now walked on with my very own feet! What a day! Found a good walking stick at the Springer Mountain Shelter. "Snake Hips," (because his wife said he hiked them off), took my picture by the bronze plaque of the "Old Hiker." My plan had been to continue on to a road at 3-Forks, 4.1 miles up the AT, but Snake Hips told me about Long Creek Falls just a little farther than 3-Forks on a side trail which would be a great place to camp. I decided to go for it. My pack was giving me trouble. I had rearranged the contents in the morning, to try the heaviest at the bottom, sleeping bag on top, instead of the heaviest in the middle as on Day 1. Think it was a mistake. Shoulders bothering and have had to take off the pack frequently. Had to stop for supper on the trail at 4:30 and later rest by a stream to wash my feet/take a spit bath. Got energized to push on to Long Creek Falls. Worth the push! I celebrated with a cold dip in the falls, fully clothed. Bath and laundry at the same time! Set up tent right at base of the falls.

I have officially completed my first northbound AT section-hike. Yay!

Wednesday, October 12, 2005

57°. Good sleep. Nothing but the roar of the falls. Will head south to Amicalola today to complete my pre-hike. I'm beginning to believe that next year's long hike is do-able. I'm loving this!

Read John 17 this morning. Amazing. Jesus was about to face his own death but prayed for his disciples and for the generations to follow. "My prayer is not for them alone, I pray also for those who will believe in me through their message." (John 17:20 New International Version) So, I believe, does that mean Jesus prayed for me? Wow.

1:45 pm 57°. Overcast but another clear view from Springer! Stopping to get water south of Black Gap where I passed on the way in. Saw another bear at 9 am crossing the path as I was coming out of Long Creek Falls beside Stover Creek. Poor things! I keep scaring them! He was just having his morning coffee and here comes a vicious hiker so, must run! This time up the hill, off the path. I met a hiker yesterday, Geezer, who said he'd hiked hundreds of miles and never saw a bear. Says nobody ever sees them. He said I should buy a lottery ticket. I'm lucky because I saw two bears...in the wild... while I'm hiking and camping alone. It's all a matter of perspective. I thought it was pretty neat, too, but maybe not everyone would think so.

I met a guy at a parking lot yesterday who was starting his first hike. When Snake Hips and his wife told about me seeing a bear he got all wide-eyed and said, "You saw a bear? I'm a New York/Florida boy!" What, you think with all the warning signs and bear cables that there are no bears? He was heading to the Stover Creek Shelter with two huge duffle bags that had to weigh 100 pounds apiece. He said he didn't want to hike alone and hoped there'd be people at the shelter. I did not volunteer to hike with him and made a quick getaway.

Found out Monday was opening day for muzzle-loader hunting and I forgot about wearing orange. Pulled some surveyor tape off a tree and tied it around my head. Surely now I don't look like a deer! Also tucked my white poncho into my bag. Wouldn't want to be mistaken for a white tail. Thought about whistling when I heard something banging a tree. We used to "drive" deer in Maine that way. Then decided it was the 200-pounder guy trying to scare off bears. Poor guy.

Looks like I'm following Geezer back to Amicalola according to the shelter register at Springer. He's messaging a friend, Captain Hook, who he was supposed to meet up with. I found the register in a metal box in a rock crevice on top of Springer Mountain. Geezer was there at 10:25 in the fog with no view. I was there at 12:20 and could see for miles. A lady hiker had been there last week and had to stay for five days because the weather was so bad.

I didn't think I'd like backtracking to my car but have enjoyed passing the sights I saw on my way in. Lots of places where I had to rest and remove my pack that second day. Glad I went back to the Day 1 arrangement this morning. No shoulder or back problem at all and I feel really good. Expected to be hurting by now. Planning to sleep at a campsite tonight. Maybe the same one? I stink. I think bears don't eat much carrion. That's why they're leaving me alone. I smell like dead stuff.

Thursday, October 13, 2005

11:05 am. On the road heading home. I didn't stay at a campsite. Felt good. Kept going. Still daylight when I arrived at Amicalola Falls. Took the short walk over to see the top of the falls, saw the sign for stairs to the base of the 729 foot falls. "Strenuous". What? How strenuous could it be? I've just climbed a bunch of mountains! I had developed an attitude. So, down the 485 steps I headed with pack and stick, assuming I'd have to climb back up. I was never so happy to see the sign at the bottom, Visitor Center, where I'd parked my car, that way...not up!

Met up with Geezer and Captain Hook. Took pictures. It was neat seeing those hikers together. Captain Hook had come up behind me earlier covered with sweat going up the hill for all he was worth. I asked if he was looking for Geezer and he was surprised, asked if I knew him. I said we'd met Tuesday and that now he was a couple of hours ahead of me. He trekked on, hoping to meet up. Exactly the reason I hike alone. This guy was not having any fun. He was beating his body, missing the sights, to make up for getting a late start. I know, "Hike your own hike."

After they left I finally SHOWERED! Along the path in I thought, "Anybody want to smell my hiking shirt? Stand down wind in the next county!" I checked out the shelter at Amicalola. Just couldn't bring myself to sleep there. Two hikers were already there with their laundry hanging in the trees. Plus I had a new thought as I walked the trail: They say the mice are bad in the shelters because of all the good things the hikers bring. They're so bad that you have to unzip all your pouches so they won't ruin your pack. I was not so squeamish about mice. I was more concerned about mouse predators. Being originally from the North where poisonous snakes are rare, I was squeamish about snakes. I thought, "If a mouse finds a tasty morsel in my pack, isn't it possible that a snake could follow him only to be discovered by my hand in the morning as he is sleeping off the mouse indulgence? No thanks." I'd take my chances beside the trail.

Anyhow, back to where I'd sleep. That's what you think about on the trail. When you'll eat and where you'll sleep. No shelter. Decided to sleep in the van in the parking lot and cook couscous over my stove for the last time. Then I saw the sign: Restaurant and Lodge. I knew about the Lodge, "Reservations Only" but, restaurant? Hmmmm. Steak? Couscous. Steak? Couscous. Ok. Let's see if the restaurant's open. Very slow waitress treated me to two relaxing hours beside a wall of windows overlooking the mountains: Prime Rib, mashed potatoes, snow peas, salad, pineapple pie, fudge cake, strawberry cake, two cups of hot coffee and six glasses of water. I didn't ration the water. Waddled out to the van and tried to sleep. Not happening. Back inside and yes, they did have a room. Treated myself to another bath and a king-sized bed. What an ending! Oh, but this was just the beginning…

PART II JOURNEY PREPARATION

Preparation for hiking forty days took from October to May. To get in shape physically, I began by walking thirty minutes a day for three days a week. That doesn't sound like much, but it was more than I had been doing. My plan was to increase gradually until I was easily walking eight miles a day on our flat Florida roads and climbing bleachers at the ballpark wearing my hiking boots and pack. I reached both goals before stepping out on the trail. Bleacher climbing had to substitute for mountain climbing so I was pleased to accomplish thirty-five stairs, carrying thirty-five pounds, thirty-five times daily for the last few weeks before the hike.

Researching and gathering the right gear was essential. I had spent about ten years prior to my hike ridding myself of stuff. After cancer and a series of hurricanes, I had a new perspective on stuff. One, I didn't want other people to have to deal with my stuff if I died. Two, I didn't want my neighbors to have to sort through my stuff after it was blown into their yard. It was strange to be in a situation where stuff meant life. I read books by hikers, spent hours online reading AT journals, examining pictures and studying packing lists. I sought out and found an AT thru-hiker, one of those heroes who had hiked the entire trail. He was at a local sporting goods store, and he became my most valued resource. He fitted me for my pack, boots, tent, mat, and sleeping bag and advised me on water treatment. A friend of a friend who had thru-hiked sold me his maps and made a Pepsi-can alcohol stove for me. I joined the Appalachian Trail Conservancy and read every word of every magazine they sent, and I also purchased some of their literature. I prayed that my preparation would be sufficient.

FOOD

Cooking and food shopping were never favorite pastimes. I certainly never shopped or planned meals for more than one or two days at a time. Well, maybe when the children were at home and the store was miles away I had to plan. But they had been gone for years and my post-kid homes were all around the block from the grocery store. Why plan? Well, forty days in the woods might be motivation.

Jeff Alt wrote a great book, *A Walk for Sunshine*. At his suggestion I would prepare seven boxes with seven days' worth of food in each. I would seal them and address them to different points along the trail with the estimated date of arrival and a statement, "Please hold for thru-hiker" clearly marked on each label. I mapped out places that looked about seven days apart so I could be there on Sundays with maybe a chance to attend church. I know I wasn't technically a thru-hiker but it wasn't cheating; it meant they would hold the box for two weeks or so. All those boxes, except for the first, I left with my daughter, Marcy, in Charleston, SC, to send at the appropriate time. Worked like a charm. Thanks, Jeff, (not that he invented mail drop boxes, of course).

Preparing the food to put in the boxes was a challenge. I had just lost a mess of weight eating a low carbohydrate/high protein diet. I hated the thought of going off the diet but somebody said you could burn 4,000 calories a day climbing up and down mountains. Some hikers told of a diet of Ramen noodles and Snickers bars. Poor me! I might have to eat a Snickers bar, my favorite!

And so, the shopping began. Where could I find sufficient carbohydrates, enough protein, minimal weight, and enough variety to avoid the dreaded, "Another brown meal" syndrome? In addition, my meal would have to be prepared and eaten in a one-pint titanium pot. Well, okay, so brown is good. I used a seal-a-meal to package each item in the smallest size possible. Then I sealed a day's worth of items into another bag. Then I packed seven sealed bags into a gallon zip-lock bag and stuffed it into my red ditty bag. Each week's bag had to weigh no more than ten pounds.

My box would have the next seven-days worth of food, spare socks, paper for journaling, pages from the next section of *The Appalachian Trail Thru - Hikers' Companion* published by the Appalachian Trail Conservancy, packs of biodegradable tissue, alcohol for my stove, lighters, and an envelope for my bounce box. I would charge my phone and camera at the library and then send them along with anything else I didn't need to my next mail drop address about a week away.

I had a plan but depended on God's design. I had to make it to my box without being delayed by injury, sickness or by getting lost. The nutritional value had to be sufficient to keep me alert and functional. I had to be able to sleep without having critters eat my food. There were so many variables over which I had no control. I was desperately aware that something I had always taken for granted was now foundational for my journey's success. I would never lose track of my total dependence on God.

Sure, I could have left the trail to shop like other hikers. Instead, I prayed over my boxes. By grace, he was listening. I was a well-fed and happy hiker. "Unless the Lord builds the house, They labor in vain who build it." (Psalm 127:1a New King James Version)

WATER

Having living water on the trail is not a good thing so I chose Aquamira water treatment to provide safe refreshment. I had reviewed many products, and chose this simple but effective system. It worked perfectly on my pre-hike: seven drops from bottle A mixed with seven drops from bottle B, wait five minutes and add to one quart of water. Let sit twenty minutes. I had learned from my mistakes and brought the correct size of Nalgene bottles. I had a place on each side of my pack that held a bottle. I would use a simple system, "Right is right." The bottle on my right would always be ready with treated water, that way I wouldn't have to wait the twenty minutes that were required for Aquamira to work. The sources for water were clearly marked on the guide I would carry but I would never drink directly. Contaminants. Oh that removing life's contaminants could be so easy.

"Let us draw near to God with a sincere heart and with the full assurance that faith brings, having our hearts sprinkled to cleanse us from a guilty conscience and having our bodies washed with pure water." Hebrews 10:22. (New International Version)

SHELTER

Deciding about sleeping arrangements was obviously an essential part of my preparation. I knew that there were shelters along the trail, built by volunteers, where hikers could sleep. I wouldn't exactly say they served as protection from the elements or wildlife. That would be an exaggeration. They would have a floor, a roof, and three walls, generally. According to my maps, they were situated so they could be reached within a day's walk. Some would have a second platform so that two layers of hikers could sleep. Most had picnic tables and fire pits.

On a cold day hikers could smell them as the trail brought them downwind of a campfire and it quickened the step. They were welcome sites. A place to rest and trade stories with the elusive trail partners. But I would only use shelters as a last resort (excuse the pun).

Plumorchard Shelter

Except for a weekly stay in town or at a hostel, I would sleep in my tent, an MSR Hubba, for privacy and because I preferred not to sleep with mice. Just about everything I read and saw on my pre-hike confirmed that most shelters had a colony of mice underneath the platform that served the purpose of cleaning up after dinner. They were not completely tame, so they would wait until the last candle was snuffed out before they started the raid, that is, unless they were really hungry in which case they'd steal from the plate as you ate.

This strategy and God's grace would keep me from unwelcome wildlife encounters in the night. "No harm will overtake you, no disaster will come near your tent." (Psalm 91:10 New King James Version)

REGISTERS

My step-mother, Marilyn Hatch, and I were camping in Virginia in May 2005 when I came across a metal band on a cement post. "Rock Spring Hut 0.1" with an arrow pointing to my right. Underneath was a funny-looking A on a stick. It was too much for me, I had to go see. I followed white marks on trees and came across a 3-sided wooden building. Inside there was a broom and a spiral notebook. People named, "Red Streak," "Red Rover," "La-Z," "D-Tour," and "FANNPACK," had written notes in it. Under one name it said, "GA-ME 05." I was intrigued. What did it all mean? Later I learned that these spiral school notebooks were in each shelter, provided by the trail volunteers, and were a wonderful communication tool for the hikers. They could be found in tubes or hanging from a hook, or tucked inside a rock crevice. But, they were valuable. Some entries were informative. (i.e., "There is no water here.") Some were entertaining. Some encouraging. Some poetic. Some artistic. All valuable. The day's thoughts of a hiker. In preparation, I gave some thought as to what sort of messages I would leave.

TRAIL NAME

I loved reading about the hikers and discovering their trail names. Most had funny stories to explain the origin of the name. A name could be assigned by fellow hikers or the hiker could choose for himself. The name would say something about an event or a characteristic. I felt I needed to choose a name that would reflect the purpose for my hike.

I often prayed that God would be glorified in everything I think, in everything I say and in everything I do. I believed that I had a choice. If I guarded my thoughts, I could improve my course. If this was to be a time of growing in dependence on God, then it would start with giving him control of my thoughts.

The song "Happy Talk" sung by Bloody Mary in Rogers and Hammerstein's musical, *South Pacific* became my theme song for making my dream of hiking the Appalachian Trail (AT) come true:

> "Happy talk, keep talking happy talk,
> Talk about things you'd like to do.
> You got to have a dream,
> If you don't have a dream,
> How you gonna have a dream come true?"

So, why did I choose the name, Happy Talk? My trail name became part of a formula which I used to sign registers:

Happy Thoughts + Happy Talk = Happy Walk.

While it might be challenging to accomplish, it was a simple formula for life's journey. "For as he thinketh in his heart, so is he." (Proverbs 23:7a King James Version)

I felt ready by the time I set foot on the trail.

PART III THE JOURNEY
GEORGIA

FROM THE JOURNEY
Saturday, 5/6/06

AMICALOLA FALLS
8.8 miles south of Springer Mt

Journal Entry: I can't believe tomorrow I'll start my forty-day hike! I'm camping with family at Amicalola Falls Campground in Georgia. Blue sky. 65°. Sunny. I learned a few things from my pre-hike last October that I'm changing for this one. I think I can finally live with my bag the way I've packed it. I have not slept well. Full of anticipation. I repacked my bag in my head last night and kept singing the, "Hey Mountain" song that I made up on my way up from Florida. I feel good about my stuff. I think I have chosen well and am grateful to my various advisors. Let's see — there was Pete for the Pepsi-can stove and maps, Critter and Byron at Travel Country for all the essentials, Eric for the monocular and knife, Barry for encouragement, Chuck for information about Georgia hiking. Lots of other encouragers and books: Trailjournals.com, *The Thru-Hiker's Handbook* by Dan "Wingfoot" Bruce, *A Walk for Sunshine* by Jeff Alt, *A Walk in the Woods* by Bill Bryson, *A Woman's Journal* by Cindy Ross and some others from the library or friends.

Marilyn picked me up in Damascus, VA, after I left my car with friends in Boone, NC. Interesting emotion yesterday on our way. We traveled the Natchez Trace and she mentioned a feeling she has when around Indian burial grounds, a connection. I fought tears coming through Birmingham. Civil rights. Almost bought a book about slavery. Connection. Eager to be on the trail. Hope I don't have to walk with people but also hope I don't have to be blunt about walking alone. Don't want to burn bridges. I think starting tomorrow, Sunday, there may fewer people on the trail.

I want a Bible with Psalms. My little pocket one only has the New Testament. I've thought of so many passages. Might use Philippians 4:8 on registers because it's about our thought-life, and I expect to have a lot of time to think.

Note to Readers: The Bible records in the Book of John, chapter 4, verse 10 that Jesus told the woman at the well that he could give her living water so that she would thirst no more. Each day's journal entry will end with a section called, "From the Well" and will record a refreshing application of the Living Word which came from my experience on the trail.

FROM THE WELL   THOUGHTS

A purpose for my time alone with God was to purify my thoughts. In my pack, I carried a plastic bag for trash. I came to think of it as those burdensome thoughts; those thoughts that weighed me down and made me stink. I grasped Philippians 4:8,9 and held on tight. I wanted to submit every thought to the light of that scripture because the verse comes with a promise: God's peace. Wow. How much peace is that?

"Finally, brethren, whatsoever things are true, whatsoever things are honest, whatsoever things are just, whatsoever things are pure, whatsoever things are lovely, whatsoever things are of good report; if there be any virtue, and if there be any praise, think on these things. Those things, which ye have both learned, and received, and heard, and seen in me, do: and the God of peace shall be with you." (Philippians 4:8,9 King James Version)

FROM THE JOURNEY   LONG CREEK FALLS
Sunday 5/7/06   4.9 miles North of Springer

Camped at Long Creek Falls where I left off my northbound section hike last fall. Family dropped me off at Springer Parking Lot/Big Stamp Gap just north of Springer Mountain, the southern terminus of the Appalachian Trail at 11 am. Headed out and found myself at the top of Springer at 11:45. Oops. I was there on my pre-hike last October! Meant to head north! Thought about changing my trail name to "Wrongway" but decided, no, this is the way I took so it is the right way! Met an old Ridgerunner and he helped me get out the feather for a picture. Signed the register, "Headed north to ...? Joy in the Journey, Happy Talk." Told the guy I planned to head north forty days and he said, "Planning to get to Damascus?" Yes! It was good to hear my goal was realistic although I secretly wondered if I'd make it out of Georgia. Seven people and two dogs showed up and they were headed north for a few days. Decided to get ahead of them.

12:15 pm Back at the parking lot. Met lots of people but managed to hike alone except for about thirty minutes with Andy, a twenty-something year old on a four-month hike. Fortunately he hiked faster so it was not a problem to persuade him to go on ahead. It was neat seeing the places I passed on my pre-hike. Enjoyed wild flowers and the hemlocks along Stover Creek, no bear this time. Cooked spinach couscous and tuna beside the falls, treated water.

Gear is working really well. Pouring rain and I'm dry. Wore my blue poncho while I cooked. It was drizzling then and easy to keep stuff covered. Ate watching for bear. Cleaned up somebody's mess — trash and orange peels around the fire pit. There was a sealable tin can so put all the stuff in, sealed it and plopped it in the river. I'll pack it out tomorrow. Thought it would reduce the odor. Couldn't finish my couscous. Packed it up. Made an attic of bandana in peak of tent and have flashlight, pepper spray and knife in it. I call it my Eric stuff. Feather in tree outside. Must sleep. Tomorrow I'll take the first steps of my second AT section hike!

FROM THE WELL   FEATHER PROTECTION

When people heard of my plan to walk forty days on the Appalachian Trail they were interested. It was a foreign thought to most of the people I knew. They were curious; they humored me while deep down inside they were sure I would not actually make the hike. I had camped but never outside a campground, never carrying a backpack and never alone. What? Alone? No! Not alone! Had I not read the reports? Had I not heard the warnings?

My response initially was that there are bears and boars and snakes and rabid things and bad mouse droppings and lunatics and treacherous trails. There are terrorists; I still fly. If I die on the trail, write on my headstone "She lived until she died." What a foolish, irresponsible thing for this grandmother to even consider. Surely I would bring a gun or a dog or a man. And, they secretly began to hope that I would not make the hike.

Corrie Ten Boom wrote in her book *Hiding Place* that she read Psalm 91 daily while in a German concentration camp. My friend read Psalm 91 daily while her son served in Iraq. They did this because they believed in the ever-present Emmanuel God. I adopted Psalm 91 as my Psalm and told the worriers to pray for feathers. I carried a feather over my shoulder attached to my pack, for protection.

[1]" Whoever dwells in the shelter of the Most High will rest in the shadow of the Almighty. [2] I will say of the Lord, 'He is my refuge and my fortress, my God, in whom I trust.' [3] Surely he will save you from the fowler's snare and from the deadly pestilence. [4] He will cover you with his feathers, and under his wings you will find refuge; his faithfulness will be your shield and rampart. [5] You will not fear the terror of night, nor the arrow that flies by day, [6] nor the pestilence that stalks in the darkness, nor the plague that destroys at midday. [7] A thousand may fall at your side, ten thousand at your right hand, but it will not come near you. [8] You will only observe with your eyes and see the punishment of the wicked. [9] If you say, 'The Lord is my refuge,' and you make the Most High your dwelling, [10] no harm will overtake you, no disaster will come near your tent." (Psalm 91:1-10 New International Version)

SECOND AT SECTION-HIKE: LONG CREEK FALLS NORTH TO… ?

FROM THE JOURNEY
Monday 5/8/06

JUSTUS CREEK
13.6 miles north of Springer

7:30 am. 60°. Overcast. Slept well, once I thought of God's light. Tried to think of hymns beginning with A,..got stuck on Q. Don't we always get stuck on Q? Feather didn't get blown away. Ready to find this new day! The first steps of my second section hike.

Rough day but found a clearing about 2:00 pm and set up the tent, crawled into my sleeping bag to rest until about 4, revived. Saw a little black garden snake. He was all lumpy and looked dead. I think that was his ploy to get this fierce predator to leave him alone, or maybe he was dealing with a mouse. I don't know much about snake ailments. I didn't want to step over him so knocked him off the trail with my pole. He lay on the side for a few seconds, no longer lumpy, then slithered away. Okay, so it was stomach cramps relieved by that little flick. Glad I could help. Saw a centipede — "How far ya goin"? "Oh, no plan beyond the other side of this path." Kindred spirits. Saw a bunny — took several pictures because he just kept letting me get closer. Saw a bluebird. Most of my pics are of the ground because I seldom looked up, therefore, few birds. Hiked until about 7 pm.

Miles hiked today on AT: 8.7

FROM THE WELL   FEAR

As I lay in my tent that first night at Long Creek Falls it was dark. Very dark. I couldn't see my hand in front of my face. I could hear the water and the woods, the breeze in the trees, the fall of a limb, the skittering of a squirrel, the break of a branch. The break of a branch? What would break a branch? Who would break a branch? How close was that branch to my tent? Why did it break? My ears grew. My eyes widened to my temples. My skin grew pimples.

I remembered the verse I taught children at a Christian school in Maine some thirty years earlier. "What time I am afraid I will trust in Thee," (Psalm 56:3. King James Version) It wasn't working. I needed to breathe, but I didn't dare. Branch-cruncher might hear me and know I was in the tent. It was part of my plan to always check out the area before getting inside my tent. Bad people could think I was a mean, ugly, strapping, fighter-guy whom they ought not to disturb. I had carefully cleaned up all hiker trash from the area as soon as I had arrived at the site so that no bear would be interested in snooping around. So, lying there I had no reason to fear the dark. I prayed.

Then I remembered, God is light; in him there is no darkness. He can see perfectly so I didn't need to. I rolled over and went to sleep, never to fear the dark on the trail again. "Even the darkness will not be dark to you; the night will shine like the day, for darkness is as light to you." (Psalm 139:12 New International Version)

FROM THE JOURNEY   PARKING LOT
Tuesday 5/9/06   26.8 miles north of Springer

7:55 am. 58°. Overcast. Slept well beside Justus Creek. Young couple camped across the creek. Onward.

Saw a sign that reminded me of the anger I'd been trying to avoid. It infuriated me that I couldn't rid my life of those thoughts. I'd be going along, happy, having happy thoughts and then, Bam! I'd be hit with those incipient reminders. Suddenly I came upon a little fence with a purple iris growing at its base. It was all by itself, just blossoming for anybody to enjoy. What a gift! I was immediately out of my funk and grateful for my life and future.

1:30 pm arrived at a parking lot. Nice place here, got rid of trash. Called Marilyn regarding my cousin David because I spent much of the day thinking of and praying for him. He used canes because of Multiple Sclerosis and I had been thinking about my trekking poles.

Looks like a real bathroom over across the road. Yay!

Found a good campsite. Feel good. Overcast and cool all day. Misty. Walking in the clouds. Cold night. Will have to dress extra tonight.

Miles hiked on AT today: 13.2

FROM THE WELL   POLE ENCOURAGEMENT

If the apostles called Barnabas, "The Son of Encouragement" would two encouragers be called "Barnabi?" There were times on the trail when the legs just screamed out, "That's enough! I'm not doing this anymore! Who's idea was this anyway?" I would try to rest them, pamper them. I used every motivational skill I knew of yet they refused to move. That's where Barnabi came in. Some would call them Leki trekking poles but that's just because they didn't know them like I did.

They were the encouragers. Barnabas on the left would step up on the impassable obstacle. He would say to my right leg, "Come on. You can do this. It is only one step and then you can rest." Right leg would believe him and take the step, only to be followed immediately by Barnabas on the right, reaching to a bad thing. He would say to the bad thing, "Is that all you've got? You think you can stop this machine? We're coming through so get outta the way!" Then, ever so gently, he'd tell left leg that the path was cleared; it was okay to advance. Another step. Another encouragement. Another step.

The Christian community is like that. There are encouragers who keep us moving forward. Sure, there are obstacles, and they are real, but they have no power to stop us. "Therefore comfort each other and edify one another, just as you also are doing, (1 Thessalonians 5:11 New International Version)

FROM THE JOURNEY   NEEL'S GAP
Wednesday 5/10/06   30.5 miles north of Springer

7:30 am Waiting for water to boil for coffee. Extra clothes sufficient last night but my stuff got wet. Hope the sun shines so I can dry out.

4:30 pm Wow. Made it to Walasiyi/Neel's Gap early in the day. Blood Mountain had large rocks to climb over but really not a problem. Sun appeared briefly in the mist. Cool all day but I was okay with insulated top and sleeveless quick-dry shirt. Lots of people on the trail. The group of seven dwindled to four and left at Neel's Gap. I showered and did laundry. Then I heard there was a thunderstorm coming so I decided to spend the night in the Hostel.

I had never slept at a hostel so I wasn't sure exactly how it worked. The man in the store said to go down, pick out a bed, and come back to pay. There were sixteen hikers planning to spend the night, only two other women. Okay. Would there be a women's section? I didn't dare ask, so I ventured down and found a room full of bunk beds. No pink sleeping bags for the ladies or blue for the men. The only available bed was at the opposite end from the two women. Top bunk in the corner. So, that would be my home for the night. I went up and purchased earplugs, just in case I or the thirteen men around me snored.

Wanted to send post cards from here but none of the pictures are right — haven't seen the views because of all the mist. Talked about my feather with a hiker who had a matching turkey feather. He said there's a hiker passage in Psalm 91 about tents. It was neat to find believers here. I learned that Psalm 91 has prophetic portions about Jesus' temptation. God is good, the way he works all things out.

Miles hiked on AT today: 3.7

FROM THE WELL   REFUGE

In order to survive several days in the woods, one has to carry sufficient gear for any weather and enough extra gear to be prepared for a prolonged stay. At the same time, if you carry too much your back, legs and feet will give out, then you won't need any of it because you'll be off the trail! By my third day on the trail, I was already hearing of hamburger feet, grateful that they weren't my own.

Somehow Tuesday night, rainwater had made its way inside my tent. My mat and sleeping bag were wet. This was serious. I knew I had to dry out before dark but there was only mist, no sun as I walked. It would be too cold to sleep while wet. I had already learned to trust God with my sleeping place, and I was praying more than ever.

My first thunderstorm was spent with a wilderness church in a stone building in dry clothes and a warm bed. "I will say of the Lord, 'He is my refuge and my fortress, my God, in whom I trust.' " (Psalm 91:2 New International Version)

FROM THE JOURNEY
Thursday, 5/11/06

LOW GAP
43.1 miles north of Springer

Stopped at a leaking rock to collect and treat water. Slept at a campsite on top of a mountain two miles north of Low Gap. Got there about 7pm after going south when I signed Low Gap register. Oops. Saw this lumpy tree that looked remarkably like one I'd taken a picture of going north...with large white quartz rocks at its base. Got out my camera and reviewed — yup — same tree! I was about forty-five minutes south of my watering spot. Headed north again — stopped in at Low Gap to share my funny hiker story with the hikers I'd met back at Neel's Gap. Took a picture. Set up camp and along came Ray who I had seen a few times along the trail. Super camping companion because he built a nice fire with wet wood, collected sassafras root and boiled up some nice sassafras tea with brown sugar for us. Hit the spot. Major wind during the night. He estimated gusts to 50 mph. I slept in long johns, purple fleece-lined jacket, silk bag liner, sleeping bag and eventually wrapped in poncho as well. Sang my "Jesus Calmed the Storm" song until I fell asleep.

Miles hiked on AT today: 12.6

FROM THE WELL

WRONGWAY

Was this becoming a pattern? How many times would I retrace my steps? I came to view these as part of God's plan. There was something he wanted me to see, somebody to meet, weather to avoid. I was enthused with new anticipation for what lay ahead, and greater trust in his plan.

"'For I know the plans I have for you,' declares the Lord, 'plans to prosper you and not to harm you, plans to give you hope and a future'" (Jeremiah 29:11 New International Version)

FROM THE JOURNEY
Friday, 5/12/06

CHEESE FACTORY
54.1 miles north of Springer

Grateful for clear skies in the morning. Late start. Didn't even get up until 8:30 and Ray boiled up a nice pot of coffee. Shared water, cup, oatmeal, Esbit tablets and were joined by Buddhist - Mathew. He's hiking to Maine barefoot with a shawl and a Bible, reading the book of John. Interesting conversation. Explained the Gospel to them but no evidence of acceptance. Looks like a good day

7:30 pm Arrived at Cheese Factory campsite with Ray. Nice fire. Hot chocolate. Probably will hike together to Hiawasee. Seem to keep the same pace. I'll get my first mail drop box there, if all goes according to plan.

Miles hiked on AT today: 11

FROM THE WELL

SASSAFRAS

The sassafras leaves had always intrigued me. How could the same tree produce leaves of such varying shapes? As children we called them mittens, gloves, and hands. They surrounded the trail as

I walked, and thus evoked thought and discussion with God. The leaf of a closed hand, with fingers together made me think of how water can be cupped in the hand for a drink. On the trail, the days consisted of thinking about where I would sleep, when I would eat, if I would find water. There is nothing more refreshing than a sip of water when it's been lacking. Such a simple thing to offer, a sip of water, yet all too often held back.

The glove leaf, with fingers extended, reminded me of an open hand, ready to work and carry another's burden. Occasionally, I would meet a hiker carrying two packs, one for an injured companion or stranger. How many times did I see evidence of outward thinking? Why is the fire pit ready for a match with nobody around? Why do the volunteers spend hours trimming bushes and moving rocks? There is no expectation of receiving anything in return, no fingers pointing back.

The mitten hand is like a handshake. A little thing, really, when we greet a stranger at church. Yet, that welcome, that warmth, may make the difference as the recipient is moved to consider his life, his needs, his eternity.

As I passed sassafras from Georgia to Virginia I had many opportunities to examine what sort of story my hands told. I was ashamed to admit, not enough. "And the King will answer and say to them, 'Assuredly, I say to you, inasmuch as you did it to one of the least of these My brethren, you did it to Me.'" (Matthew 25:40 New King James Version)

FROM THE JOURNEY   HIAWASSEE
Saturday 5/13/06   66.6 miles north of Springer

8:30 am Only been hiking thirty minutes but couldn't pass up this spot. Huge rock cliff with great view of the mountain I'm about to climb (Tray?) and ranges as far as the eye can see. I can't count all the different bird songs I'm hearing, but they're VERY happy. Blue sky, sun shining bright. Life is good. Nice campsite last night and perfect temperature but minimal sleep. Thought I could hear somebody's stomach growling outside my tent and wondered if Mathew was weirder than he seemed. Lots of activity from vehicles on the dirt road nearby, people arguing, dog barking. Hunkered down in my tent under rhododendrons, I hoped they'd all go away. Got up expecting Ray to be gone but his tent was still there. Made my breakfast and coffee and he got up and started his. He may go off on his own now but that's okay. He's a little bit distracting from my walk with God. I don't like to have to plan according to another person, for example, I would not have chosen this site so close to a road. He seems okay with giving me space. He was an interesting companion and useful for a campfire!

Ray, three men and I had been walking about the same pace all Saturday. Most difficult day yet. Was anxious to know how I'd get to Hiawassee. The first mail drop for supplies was scheduled to be waiting for me at the post office in Hiawassee a week after I left Springer. I hoped to be there before they closed on Saturday. I planned to arrive, find a place to camp, attend church on Sunday, and then return to the trail Monday. The plan was a good one, I thought, except for the minor detail that I hadn't planned for the eleven miles of road from the trailhead to town. Being a female solo hiker, hitchhiking was not an option. Walking an extra eleven miles was not an option. Decided to stay with the three men because it was a sure thing. Their truck was at the Dick's Creek parking lot and they weren't prepared to spend the night. Left Ray who was deciding about Deep Gap Shelter and going on ahead, heard there might be bad weather. The men thought they'd be done by 3 o'clock, turned out it took until 6 pm. I was able to reach Ellen's friend by phone but she was not open to a visitor, even on her lawn, "A limb might fall on you," so she suggested Macedonia Baptist Church, Harold Ledford, Pastor. No phone number or address for the friend's church, which would be closed on a Saturday afternoon anyway. So, Lord, what's the plan? Meeting the three men with a truck seemed like a great answer. My plan was to be dropped off at MacDonald's for an apple salad and then find the number for the church. Maybe the pastor would let me camp in the yard and use an outdoor faucet to rinse off the trail grunge.

But then, what was that? Was that the church she mentioned? Quickly I banged on the roof of their truck and bailed out into the parking lot. Strangers were coming out from a wedding. I approached a man, asked if he knew if the pastor was around, told him I wanted to work for tent spot and outdoor faucet. Instead, Dale and Sue brought me to their home and gave me a beautiful guest room! They said I could stay and they would bring me to the post office, library and trailhead on Monday. Maybe there was a reason for the "wrongway" back down the trail, or for the time I sat on that rock this morning.

Miles hiked on AT today: 12.5

Sunday, 5/14/06   Dale and Sue's

Mother's Day. They brought me to their church and Sue approached the pastor to ask if I could share my journey. He interviewed me in his office and said he'd make time for me. Planned to end with the song but a family had two songs and gave testimonies so I decided I should keep it short. People seemed to enjoy it and were responsive. Back to the house for Beef Burgundy, green beans, creamed potatoes, sliced tomatoes, salad, rolls, coffee, fruit and cool whip. Yum. She's going to give me her recipe for pineapple casserole. Wonderful people, great home. Awesome God! "For I was hungry and you gave Me food; I was thirsty and you gave Me drink; I was a stranger and you took Me in." (Matthew 25:35 New King James Version)

FROM THE WELL   RESUPPLYING

A new thought. A mail drop box is like a Sunday. It is interesting that my plan was to be at a location to be resupplied on Sundays. My commitment to a daily walk with the Lord has been inconsistent through my Christian life but not the observance of Sundays as a day for worship and fellowship, a filling up, so to speak. I always knew I needed this time to resupply. My box needed filling in order to go on for another week.

It was God's design to do his good work for six days and then rest on the seventh. He commanded that we do the same. The system is built into us in order to keep us full.

FROM THE JOURNEY   WHEELER KNOB (CAMPSITE)
Monday, 5/15/06   73.2 miles north of Springer

It was good to get back on the trail. There were three hikers at Dick's Creek - a couple doing four more days and a thru hiker, Danger, but I hiked alone. I saw them again at Plum Orchard shelter when I signed in and had supper. It looked like a full house.

They had seen Ray and Mathew within the last couple of days. Mathew was last seen laying beside the road to Hiawassee. I prayed he'd be okay and open to Christ. Betty, 70's, showed up and she'd been with Ray a while. She knows mutual friends from Florida Trail Association (FTA) from a Loxahatchee hike, 1998. I left the shelter to go a couple more hours. I felt good and weather was perfect. Flowers marked the path for me. Couldn't find the right spot and made two searches into the woods to find a place to put up the tent and kept praying God would give me a good safe place. Awesome answer!

8:30 pm Came across the best site so far. Rock furniture, flat. I was full of gratitude and praise. Burst out in song, but had to keep it down a little! Can't believe I'll make the border tomorrow!

Miles hiked on AT today: 6.6

FROM THE WELL   FLOWERS

Walking the trail in May and June I saw mostly rocks, roots and flowers. It was rare to see much of anything else because it was not wise to look up, away from the next step. I covenanted with God when I saw my first flower on the trail. Certain flowers and colors reminded me of people I knew. I promised to pray for those people as he placed the flowers on my path. For example, Lady Slippers reminded me of my daughters. Violets reminded me of mothers in my life.

Yellow flowers reminded me of my two blond friends and their families. One day, some sort of yellow flower surrounded me and I spent an hour or so praying for my friends. Later, I learned that one son had been in a motorcycle wreck and a dear friend had died in a car accident.

Trillium became my companion. There is a certain variety with three white petals and red centers, the Painted Trillium. I began to think of these as reminders of the trinity, so that as I walked and came across one, I would spend the next several miles thinking and praying about the trinity, and what each part of it meant to me.

The green leaves made me think of the Creator God, the white petals represented the Holy Spirit, and the red center told of the Christ who's shed blood paid the penalty for my sin. Isaiah referred to the newborn child as Emmanuel, meaning, God with us. Exactly. Jesus lived on earth among mankind for thirty-three years. His sinless life and subsequent death and resurrection guaranteed eternal life for believers. But what is this, eternal life? Pie in the sky, by and by? Something we don't get until we die? How foolish! Yet, to many, Jesus is nothing more than protection against eternity in Hell.

The flowers called out to me, "Emmanuel! Emmanuel! I am with you, not just at death, not just for eternity after death, but now, here, at this very moment and every moment to come!" Since I came to faith in Christ he had been my constant companion, and though my senses were dull to his presence, he was there, he is here, he will be there. It strikes me as amazing that we can live moment to moment with God. "Jesus Christ the same yesterday, and today, and for ever." (Hebrews 13:8 King James Version)

NORTH CAROLINA

FROM THE JOURNEY
Tuesday, 5/16/06

STANDING INDIAN SHELTER
83.1 miles north of Springer

So, I just walked from Georgia to North Carolina! My first border crossing! Cool tree to welcome me. Took its picture. Trees are good. They tell stories. Really went slow today. Staying at campsite at Standing Indian Shelter. Several young adult Christians. Can't write — tired! Going well.

Miles hiked on AT today: 9.9

FROM THE WELL   TREE SPEAK

Mr. Flute was an interesting creation. He was probably beautiful and served his purpose in his youth but now he stood there, playing his joyful tune to the Lord while bugs and woodpeckers did their thing.

Nose Tree had been lying about how easy it was to hike in the mountains and so his nose had grown long with deformity.

Rock Tree stood as an encourager to any passerby. You could not miss the determination. Yes, the seed had been planted on a rock but that didn't sway him; well, not much. Add a little dust, a splash of moisture, a bit of sunshine and in time, you have a tree. I leaned on him for a few moments just to let him know I appreciated and heard his message. "I can do all things through Christ who strengthens me." (Philippians 4:13 New King James Version)

"For you shall go out with joy, and be led out with peace; the mountains and the hills shall break forth into singing before you, and all the trees of the field shall clap their hands. " (Isaiah 55:12 New King James Version)

FROM THE JOURNEY   BIG BUTT MOUNTAIN
Wednesday, 5/17/06   95.6 miles north of Springer

Who named this mountain? Reminds me of Chunky Gal a few miles back. Walked, drank, ate, slept, time passed. Feeling weighed down. Lots of time to think.

Miles hiked on AT today: 13.5

FROM THE WELL   MOUNTAIN MESSAGES

"Hey Mountain, what's your name?
Have you secrets, what's your game?
Will you leave me whole or lame?
Hey Mountain, what's your name?"

It was a simple song that I thought of as I crested a hill and saw distant mountains from a highway in Georgia. I wondered which ones I would climb, what sort of adventures I would have, if I would be able to continue or be defeated. I was committed to forty days but would I spend them all in Georgia? I carried portions of *The Appalachian Trail Thru-Hikers' Companion*. It was helpful for knowing my approximate location and proximity to water, roads, and towns. I gauged my progress by it and would make notes when I arrived at various points along the way. But I seldom knew the name of the mountains that loomed around me or how far it was to the top of the one I was on.

Peaks and valleys often mark life's journey. Sometimes a mountain refers to a negative experience. Something like a hurdle to get over and move on. Other times a mountain refers to those highlights in life, those mountaintop experiences.

I began to consider the mountains in my life. How had they left me? Did they have a purpose? If I truly believed God was alive and involved with every detail of my life, had I missed the message of the mountains? I resolved to trust God with all my mountains. "And we know that all things work together for good to those who love God, to those who are the called according to His purpose." (Romans 8:28 New King James Version)

FROM THE JOURNEY
Thursday, 5/18/06

WINDING STAIR GAP
106.6 miles north of Springer

Albert Mountain today. What a climb! Stairs and more stairs. Had to set my pack up ahead of me to climb up rock. Hiked down to Wasilik Poplar yesterday — long steep walk. Big tree. Fence around, missing plaque. Thunder and dark skies in the afternoon and didn't want to cross the road late because others would know I would have to camp nearby. Slept well. No storm. Stealth camped just south of US 64, Franklin.

Miles hiked on AT today: 10

FROM THE WELL

NARROW PATH

My senses were alive there in the woods. My thoughts were busy. The people were interesting. There was much to entertain me and fill my days, but occasionally when the path was wide, level, and smooth, I would close my eyes and rest while I walked. Of course, eventually I would stumble. Interesting. When the path was narrow and rocky I was focused, preparing each step, being careful not to turn an ankle or fall. But, on the broad path, I became complacent.

Life can be like the broad path. Sometimes we adopt the "everybody's doing it" mentality. If we are broad-minded enough, we may accept that morality is not so defined. It could be different for each member of society. There are no absolutes. All is relative. Yet, what is legal or acceptable may not necessarily be right or good for our society. Years ago my pastor preached a series of sermons on the Ten Commandments. He taught us not just what is forbidden, but also what is permitted. He showed us the loving, protective Father whose discipline enhances life. I discovered there is freedom in following God's design. Complacency can conceal the borders. "Enter through the narrow gate. For wide is the gate and broad is the road that leads to destruction, and many enter through it. But small is the gate and narrow the road that leads to life, and only a few find it." (Matthew 7:13,14 New International Version)

FROM THE JOURNEY   BARTRAM TRAIL
Friday, 5/19/06   114.7 miles north of Springer

Haven't seen anybody else so far. Took a side trail to Siler Bald Shelter then followed the AT to Siler Bald. Lone tree on top of hill. Sang "How Great Thou Art" by Carl Boberg — wept prayers. Very good time near to God. Sang "Old Rugged Cross" by George Bennard and thought about the cross and all that it means, what Christ experienced, sweet time.

Miles hiked on AT today: 7.7

FROM THE WELL   TREE ON A HILL

It was a narrow path over a barren hill, Siler Bald. From the bottom I could see a lone tree silhouetted against a blue sky. It's hard to write about my thoughts of that day. I felt compelled. I had been alone all day, one of the few days that I saw no other hikers. Free of distractions and particularly sensitive to God's presence, I wept as I climbed the path. I thought of Jesus, stumbling up Golgotha, bearing his cross, my sin. The lone tree at the top represented the tree from which my Savior hung, bearing the shame for sin that wasn't his.

When I got to the top, I could see miles of mountains. The beauty was breathtaking. My heart feels tight in my throat even now as I write of it because I have never felt closer to God. Songs of praise poured out of me. Verses I don't recall memorizing ran across my mind. Prayers flowed like a spring river.

I don't know how many hours I sat there. I just know I never wanted to leave. I wish the picture I took could have captured the heart. I hope my mind never loses its memory of that day, that place, that God. "And he said to them all, 'If any man will come after me, let him deny himself, and take up his cross daily, and follow me. '" (Luke 9:23 King James Version)

FROM THE JOURNEY   WESSER BALD
5/20/06 Saturday   127.4 miles north of Springer

Noon. Stopped at a stream north of Wayah Bald. Misty like Springer. Thunder and Lightening (T&L) last night at campsite south of Wayah. Slept well remembering God's protection. Alone all day. Don't know where I'll worship tomorrow — maybe on a mountain, maybe evening service at Wesser. Hope so. Will have to buy food at Nantahala Outdoor Center, — not enough to get to Fontana. Work crew here to build shelter near Wayah - two locals I met, others from VA. Thanked them.

8:30pm I think I'm on Wesser Bald - T&L but I couldn't go on. Set up just before the rain — prayed Jesus hold storm back. Others got hail and lightening all around! Prayed Psalm 91 in tent. Right knee and foot pain gone after prayer. Eight students at Cold Spring Shelter.

Miles hiked on AT today: 12.7

FROM THE WELL   PAIN

When I was sixteen, I was skiing in deep powder some place in Vermont. I turned my right knee but was able to get down the mountain although in pain. Over the course of my life the knee pain would flare up, usually to let me know it needed a rest. It was never a problem, really. I don't know if that old injury was the culprit these many years later. One morning, I woke up unable to straighten my right leg without excruciating pain. I figured it was just the way I had been laying on it, so I gave it some time and eventually it eased up. A few days later, it occurred again as I was walking, but again, eased up with rest.

A third time, my right leg screamed. It was about noon some place in North Carolina. I rested it, massaged it, raised it up, snacked, drank water, but found no relief. Each step the pain increased until it finally began taking my breath away if I put any pressure on it at all. It made my eyes water so that I couldn't see the trail.

I determined that I would have to find a way to put my tent up where I stood because I could not take another step. Before setting my pack down I prayed. I told God that if he wanted me to stop my hike, if I had accomplished what he had in mind for me to do, then I would find my way off the mountain the next morning and thank him for the experience. But if he intended for me to continue, then please, fix what's wrong, take away the pain and let me go on. My next step didn't hurt, and it never gave me a problem again on the trail. I realized I had been trying to fix the problem myself. How foolish. "Casting all your care upon Him, for He cares for you," (1 Peter 5:7 New King James Version). "You do not have because you do not ask." (James 4:2c New King James Version)

8:15 pm Here I sit in the community room at NOC waiting for my Sharpa Veggies and chicken to heat up in the microwave, fresh apple and a blackberry cobbler neatly arranged at my table waiting for the last bite of the main course. Soaked my feet in the Nantahala. Showered forever, washed clothes. Made my bunk up in my cabin and fashioned a window screen. Life is good.

Lydia has a friend, Alan, who will pick me up at 9:00 am at the restaurant to take me to Fontana. I'm skipping a section to get my re-supply box and chargers. Tipped over my pack at a spring and soaked my camera. It works if I take out the battery, put it back in and snap a shot quickly. I'm hoping, praying, it's okay and re-charging will solve the problem. Otherwise will have to carry throw-aways. Hope not. Broke my monocular second or third day out because I attached it to my poles for getting it quickly. Guess it couldn't take the pounding.

Made calls to family and Jan. Will meet her and Pat, Florida friends, at Grayson Highlands north of Damascus, VA, at the end of the hike for sure even if I have to skip more trail. They'll be bringing me back to my car in Boone, NC. I'm not a "purist" when it comes to hiking the AT, it's not about passing every white blaze. I made that decision when I missed 0.9 miles of trail taking the loop to Siler Bald Shelter. Well-worth the experience and the register entry to "Bryce" — somebody's grandson who will receive the register when it's full. Then the hike up Siler - awesome.

Really pushed last night to find a place to sleep. That's always the hardest time — where will I sleep? Prayed a lot for a safe place because of the T&L. Had to stop at a place that didn't look safe — top of a mountain. Picked the most sheltered place I could find and struggled to sit up in my tent to get the nighttime things done. Bad dreams again. I guess it's the only place Satan can attack, I have no control. Well, I know he could attack in other ways, praise God for protection. Maybe it's something I'm eating — have had three nights with bad dreams. Once it had something to do with Connie and another was of something rubbing against the outside of my tent along my side. I was so scared, in my dream, and I couldn't make a noise. Finally a low "w-a-h!" came out and I woke myself up. Nothing there, of course.

I jumped three deer one night, only saw the white flag of one, saw three grey squirrels today, one dead mole, rabbit, snails, caterpillars, butterflies, Towhees, hawk, Juncos, and lots of flowers. I stop, look behind and listen often but no sign of bears. Used toe warmers one night and had to light a fire in the vestibule to warm up, otherwise bag is working great. Tent soaks through if it's been wet for several days. Only happened once. I can usually dry it out by laying it out in the sun on the trail. Back usually hurts by bed time, toes usually painful as soon as I lay down — somewhat of a problem because it keeps me awake. Sometimes I change to my camp shoe sandals if it's too bad.

8:50 pm Guess I'll turn in. Full belly. Things to do in the cabin to be sure I'm ready for my ride. Feel very good and am happy. This is a very good trip — looking forward. "Do not be anxious about anything, but in every situation, by prayer and petition, with thanksgiving, present your requests to God." (Philippians 4:6 New International Version)

Miles hiked on AT today: 6.4

FROM THE WELL   HIGH TECH

Can we expect more from God than water, food and shelter? When he promised abundant life, did he have the American Dream in mind? In our present culture, we have gone from wanting bigger and better to expecting smaller and faster. If our thumbs get tired from texting, we think we need a new thumb-thing or something.

My hike was very high-tech. I carried a cell phone, turned on weekly when I obtained my mail drop box. It allowed me to put my family's fears to rest. My camera was a little Canon Power Shot with a couple of extra Lithium battery packs. I had two Leki trekking poles instead of sticks. My journal consisted of seven 5"x7" pieces of paper which I kept with a pencil inside a zipper plastic bag along with the appropriate pages from *The Appalachian Trail Thru-Hikers' Companion*. There would be seven more pieces of paper in each mail drop box. My battery chargers were in the bump box that I kept mailing ahead. That's it.

I wondered how long it would take to become wasteful again. For six weeks, I had access to a shower once a week. That meant bathing beside a stream or in my tent using a bandana. I carried two one-liter bottles that needed to be refilled and treated when water was available. I never ran water while I brushed my teeth or let it run until it became hot or cold. I had two shirts and two pairs of pants that I rinsed in water collected from a creek and draped on my back to dry until I could get to the weekly hostel for laundry. I used a cut-off liter soda bottle for washing, which doubled as a container for my tent poles so they didn't dig into my pack pocket. I didn't smell or look worse than anybody else. It certainly is a ponderous thing that all my past comforts were necessary. It may take an occasional mission trip to snap me back to reality, yes, reality. I do not believe this is the intended abundant life. "I am come that they might have life, and that they might have it more abundantly." (John 10:10b King James Version)

FROM THE JOURNEY   FONTANA HILTON
5/22/06 Monday   162.6 miles north of Springer

6:45 pm Different day - I got a ride from Wesser to Fontana with Lydia's friend Alan. I purchased my back country permit and got mail. Nice cards, goodies, and some money from Rusty. I sent "Been there, Done that," post cards marked to Tennessee, tried to get a ride to Cherokee or Gatlinburg. I'm anxious about Great Smokey Mountain National Park (GSMNP) shelter restrictions and the change I will have to make in my hiking. The permit will signify me as a long-distance hiker making me eligible to tent beside the shelter but only if it is full. No more sleeping when I'm tired, stopping when I want. I understand the restrictions because of the popularity of the area, but I'll be glad to get above Davenport where I'll be free to resume the "privacy" of the woods. I hung out at the Visitor Center for a long time, back and forth to village hoping to get a ride and finally went to bed at "Hilton" — heard mice and moved in the dark to set up tent on a hill.

Miles on AT skipped: 35.2

FROM THE WELL   BORDERS

When I get to hike in the Smokies I'll have one foot in Tennessee and the other in North Carolina. What a hoot. It's been interesting, crossing borders. In Georgia, it was a weathered 2x4 nailed about eye-high on a tree with NC/GA carved in it. At Newfound Gap the border was marked in the middle of the parking lot with a painted line: Tennessee on the left, North Carolina on the right. I don't remember where Tennessee left North Carolina. It was exciting to come upon a post on the side of the trail with TN/VA carved into it. It was easy to miss the border crossings. There were no flashing neon signs. No "Welcome to the _____ State" with pictures of the state flower and a greeting from the governor.

It makes me think of life's borders. I have tried to guide my kids or grandkids by talking about drawing a line. Where should it be placed? At what point will you say, "I go this far, no farther." Will it be a line that you move or would it be written with permanent marker. And, there's such a difference between those lines that are made for you and those, in maturity, that you make for yourself.

There's lots said about living in our "comfort zones," like it's a bad thing to stay there. I'm out of that zone on this hike, yet I'm staying within the borders I have set. I have celebrated the borders, when I was aware of them. I'm not ashamed to say I love the security I find within the borders that surround me. Borders are good.

NORTH CAROLINA/TENNESSEE

FROM THE JOURNEY   ICEWATER SPRING SHELTER
Tuesday, 5/23/06   206.6 miles north of Springer

Got a ride (skipping trail by getting a ride is is called "yellow blazing") with an older couple from a Texaco at Fontana Lake to a fork in the road to Robbinsville. Then to Cherokee via a lady who was going out for tomato seeds (Stecoah to Bryson City). She drove me all the way to Cherokee and wouldn't accept money. Tried to get a ride from Cherokee to Newfound Gap by hanging around MacDonald's, then gas station, souvenir store. Finally, a lady who drives shuttle Cherokee to Gatlinburg two days a week picked me up after seeing me beside the road. Drove me there around 2 pm. Crowded with tourists. So good to be back on the trail. Eleven people here at Icewater Spring shelter. Twelve is the limit and it says no tenting. I'm going to tent, but I'll set up later. Somebody has collected wood for fire — looking forward to that. Two other women, the rest men. All cooking various dinners over various stoves. Looked like an outfitter store in the shelter. Beautiful blue sky — clear, cool. I think I'll sleep well. Looks like I can get to Standing Bear Farm real early - or go r-e-a-l slow and stay at shelters. We'll see how the traveling goes. It's hard to gauge — if I go past shelters and the trail is difficult, I'll have to push on to the next. Getting to the hostel early would be good because next one is one hundred miles away. Hmm. Charlie's Bunyan tomorrow! Can't wait!

Miles of AT skipped: 31 Miles hiked on AT today: 3

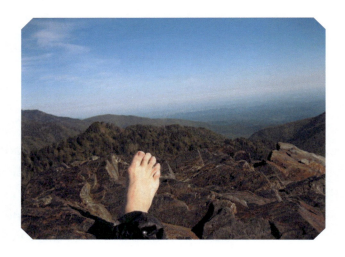

FROM THE WELL   FEET

There is nothing that gets more attention, nothing more talked about at the shelters than feet. A man even hiked the entire trail blind, but he had feet. I heard about a wheelchair accessible privy in Virginia, but there had to be feet involved to get anywhere near the shelter. Essential, yes, but I have always thought feet were a little funny.

I was the youngest of five children, which may be the reason for my round toes. They were often crammed a few extra years into my sister's old Buster Browns, so they don't lie out nice and straight. The littlest toes, in particular, suffered for space and took over some of fourth toe's room.

One night as I was inspecting my feet before tucking them in, I noticed fourth left toenail was a little discolored, thinking about turning black. It used to be a whiner, always complaining, "Not enough room!" Now there was a mark of honor for the little guy! You see, when you spend hours clumping down hills, eventually your feet move up to the front of your boot and your toes attempt to climb out. Of course, that's impossible if you're wearing good boots. This little piggie likely had no idea that only REAL hikers get black toenails! I couldn't wait to get out on the trail to brag about my black toe. I anticipated the response, "Wow! We don't have ours yet!" I would hike on with my head held a little higher, well, maybe not. I'd probably stub the dumb thing and the nail would fall off.

There is a rock formation north of Newfound Gap in the Smokey Mountains called Charlie's Bunion. I knew it was coming and was excited to see it. You see, my bunion was an important player in my trail preparation days. In case you don't know, bunions are those boney places just at the joint of the big toe. While all the other toes are pointing, "This way!", bunions have a mind of their own and prefer to move the toe at right angles. And because they're doing their own thing for which they are not designed they do not have the nice padding required for the rubbing places.

In preparation for this, my boots made many visits to the store for stretching exercises in order to accommodate Bunion. He gets capitalized because he is important. During my training days and into my first two weeks of hiking he got the special attention of New Skin applied every morning.

If he had wanted to, he could have ended my trip, so the pampering was worth it. Soon the day would come. Together we would meet the famed Charlie's Bunion. I already had the Kodak moment planned. However, when I arrived at the scene, somebody was taking a nap on Charlie and I had to wait my turn. Finally, the guy climbed down and we climbed up. I disrobed Bunion and held him just so. Perfect. Both bunions in the same shot. I devised a scheme to make money in town: people could pose for a photo op with Bunion and save the trip to the mountains. Huh. No takers. Humor aside, I was grateful for my feet and was reminded of several scriptures relating to feet and an old song about being a sermon in shoes.

"The eye cannot say to the hand, 'I don't need you!' And the head cannot say to the feet, 'I don't need you!' On the contrary, those parts of the body that seem to be weaker are indispensable, and the parts that we think are less honorable we treat with special honor. And the parts that are unpresentable are treated with special modesty." (1 Corinthians 12:21-23 New International Version)

FROM THE JOURNEY   TRI-CORNER KNOB SHELTER
5/24/06   219.2 miles north of Springer

Walked in downpour much of the day. Glad for my poncho. Didn't dampen my spirits. Hikers hunkered down in shelter. Set up nearby. Snug as a bug.

Miles hiked on AT today: 12.6

FROM THE WELL   RAIN

My family was discouraged for me as they dropped me off and my daughter reported, "It was rainy and foggy, but her spirits were far from damp." In fact, I seem to recall rudely telling them to get going so I could start my hike. I was more concerned about them driving back down the mountain.

Walking in a cool mist or rain was really not a bad thing. It was better than being hot. I knew about layering my clothing so I was comfortable and dry most of the time. It didn't matter how cold it was in the morning, because I was always shedding clothing within thirty minutes of starting my daily hike.

There was a running controversy when I was purchasing gear: To poncho or not to poncho? That was the question. I opted for the poncho although I had a North Face rain jacket as well. What a useful thing, the poncho. It was long, down to my knees. Eventually, I devised a way to attach it to the outside of my pack so that it worked as a pack cover. I could pull out the hood to cover my head without having to wear the whole thing. Many times, I spread it on the ground to lie on for a midday nap. It was a tarp to set things on as I repacked on wet mornings. I really don't know what the controversy was about; who would not want a poncho?

My journal entries usually started with a brief description of the weather. It took me a while to figure out that my thermometer wasn't working when I made my pre-hike. How could it always be fifty-seven degrees? There were many notations of "T&L." That meant thunder and lightning. I found those storms fascinating in the mountains. The trail led up, down, and around in such a way that I would think I was heading directly into a storm, and then I would be walking under clear skies with the storm behind me. The cycle would be repeated all day. Sometimes I'd get wet, sometimes not. The rain meant water for my bottles. No dampened spirits. I would trust God to accomplish his purpose, even in the rain.

> As the rain and the snow
> come down from heaven,
> and do not return to it
> without watering the earth
> and making it bud and flourish,
> so that it yields seed for the sower and bread for the eater,
> so is my word that goes out from my mouth:
> It will not return to me empty,
> but will accomplish what I desire
> and achieve the purpose for which I sent it.
> (Isaiah 55:10-11 New International Version)

TENNESSEE

FROM THE JOURNEY
5/25/06

DAVENPORT GAP SHELTER
234 miles north of Springer

When I reached Davenport Gap in Tennessee, it was pouring rain. The shelter rested on a narrow shelf on the side of a mountain. There was a chain link gate that covered the open side, protecting weary hikers from bears that had lost their fear of humans. Two platforms of men had claimed their spots — three below and three above. It seemed like the most sensible thing to sleep inside the cage with the six men whom I'd met along the trail, though I dreaded the mouse parade. Food bags hanging everywhere. Ramen noodles were spilling from pots down to the next level.

At about ten o'clock the guy singing "Red River Valley" had finished the last chorus. Then the clatter of cookware and rustle of food bags began. Something ran across me. I burrowed deep inside my bag, cinched the top closed, and folded it over so nothing could get inside. Of course, this also included fresh air. This was going to be a rough night. I prayed.

Suddenly from off in the woods came the sound of men hollering. They sounded drunk. I began to plan where I would sleep if they came to stay. It turned out that they were eleven men on horseback who were totally lost but determined to find the road. I was sorry for the horses but relieved when they were redirected to the trail.

The good news was that after they left the mice were gone, chased off by the cavalry. Journal entry: "Slept in a cage with six men. Mice arrived but somebody called the cavalry. Mice gone. Felt safe. Slept well."

Miles hiked on AT today: 14.8

FROM THE WELL   CAVALRY

The picture was a joke for the grandsons. When I was posing I had no way of knowing what I would face that night in the shelter. With all my weapons, I was grateful for answered prayer. "You will not fear the terror of night, nor the arrow that flies by day, nor the pestilence that stalks in the darkness, nor the plague that destroys at midday." (Psalm 91: 5,6 New International Version)

FROM THE JOURNEY   STANDING BEAR HOSTEL
5/26/06   237.3 miles north of Springer

Got to Standing Bear. Nice place and I was able to resupply from my drop box, which greeted me right on time. Thank you, Marcy! I was blessed to be given the privacy of the "Honeymoon Cabin" by myself instead of the bunkhouse.

Some young hikers were taking time off from the trail and partied and "fire danced" until late at night. My partying days had been over for decades and I was tired. One got up to relieve himself, obviously disoriented, followed a cable, wandered into my cabin and crawled into my bed. Fortunately, I was up packing and redirected him to his own bunkhouse. "Are you sure?" etc.

Miles hiked on AT today: 3.3

FROM THE WELL   SWITCHBACKS

What a funny way to travel. Somebody asked if I would carry a compass. What on earth for? If you go straight for any length of time, you beg for a corner. Switchbacks are the hiker's best friends. But still, it's a humorous way to travel. You literally meet yourself coming and going.

Switchbacking is essential because the side of a mountain is too steep to climb, so you zigzag back and forth, making slight incline increases as you go. It takes longer, you go farther, but the point is that you get there.

Sometimes you can see the zigzags, and it may be tempting to charge off the trail, particularly when it is downhill. You could make great progress, but at what cost? You may damage more than the environment. I saw a bear do it once, and he stumbled and somersaulted all the way down. He'd have been safer facing the vicious hiker.

Of course, I looked for the Lord in the switchbacks and he was easy to find. Repentance. It means to turn from one direction and completely turn to go in another. The comparison only goes so far because with repentance you should not return repeatedly to the original direction. That's where grace comes in because we do, and he forgives us and guides us back. "For I do not do the good I want to do, but the evil I do not want to do—this I keep on doing." (Romans 7:19 New International Version)

FROM THE JOURNEY   ROARING FORK SHELTER
5/27/06   252.7 miles north of Springer

Met Mike on trail and we hiked together until 8:30pm and stayed at Roaring Fork shelter. I camped. Good Christian fellowship.

Miles hiked on AT today: 15.4

FROM THE WELL   TRAIL MAGIC

I had heard of Trail Magic but did not expect to witness any first hand. Trail Magic are those gracious acts provided by trail supporters that help long-distance hikers to keep on keeping on. Walking along, there would be Cokes in a stream, or approaching a road, one would smell hamburgers cooking on a grill. Thru-hikers planning to complete the entire trail from Georgia to Maine, or southbound, had to leave earlier in the year. It would be a rare hiker who could leave Springer in May and get to Katahdin before the park closed in November.

One day I was hiking with a man, and we had been encouraging each other to keep going just a little farther. We were sharing scriptures and singing songs to pass the time. I was often ready to quit hiking by four in the afternoon, but we were still on the trail at seven-thirty. I wanted to stop but there wasn't a good place to camp. About to give in, I flopped down to rest and puff out a prayer for strength. We pushed up a little hill and discovered a plastic bag with Cokes and fresh oranges on a rock. Trail Magic! Right there on Max Patch at the end of May! It gave me the strength I needed to keep going until we found a safe place to stay.

As I lay in my tent I thought about God's Trail Magic. How many packages had I missed? How many did I receive but never acknowledge? Oh God, let me never take your grace for granted. "But my God shall supply all your need according to his riches in glory by Christ Jesus." (Philippians 4:19 King James Version)

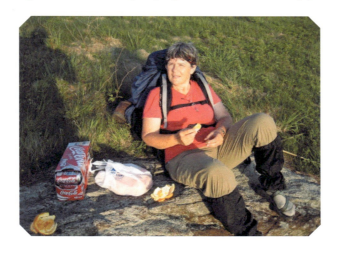

FROM THE JOURNEY   WALNUT MTN SHELTER
Sunday, 5/28/06   257.7 miles north of Springer

Had "church" this morning, now Mike's off toward Hot Springs.

Miles hiked on AT today: 5

FROM THE WELL   GIFTS

The huge outcropping of rock on the side of the mountain seemed the perfect place for lunch, a nap and a few minutes in the Word. I was reading from the first chapter of the Book of John and was struck by a new thought. God used Jesus to create. It said, "All things were made by him." I heard once that deer don't see colors as humans do. Wow.

Jesus had designed man to have colored vision; then he painted the world for us to enjoy. I mean, when I passed that flaming azalea back there, way out in the woods, away from the path where nobody could have deliberately planted it, I wondered, why is that there? Who will enjoy its beauty? Well, I noticed it, thought about it, and enjoyed it. What if it had just blended in with the surrounding browns? I would have passed it by like so many others.

It just so happened that I remembered the bush because it had appeared when I was leaning on my poles, working up strength to keep going. I had begun to think of the trail flowers as gifts, and there it was. It said, "Remember I am with you. I know your needs. I am your strength. Lean on me." If anyone could be aware of all the gifts bestowed on his children by our Heavenly father we would be overwhelmed. "If you, then, though you are evil, know how to give good gifts to your children, how much more will your Father in heaven give good gifts to those who ask him!" (Matthew 7:11 New International Version)

FROM THE JOURNEY   DEER PARK SHELTER
Monday, 5/29/06   267.5 miles north of Springer

Camped at Deer Park Mountain Shelter. Nobody else there — tented. Nasty shelter. Blister Bill stopped by but went on to the Springs. Restful night. Spent lots of the day thinking about what I'll say when I give the AT presentation to my church back home. Glad I wrote down thoughts as I went along.

Miles hiked on AT today: 9.8

FROM THE WELL   BURDENS

I recalled sermons warning about a root of bitterness. I knew about the destructive force of anger. I had been able to avoid it for most of my life; in fact, it would take a lot for me to become angry. Sometimes though, I gave in to it foolishly and uncontrollably, which made me all the more determined to avoid it.

Forty days alone on the Appalachian Trail may sound drastic, but it was my way of dealing with a root of bitterness that had sprung up within me, unwelcome, unplanned, unwanted. It was an obstacle in my path that was immovable. No, not immovable, because it was pushing me backwards.

My pack weighed twenty-five to thirty-five pounds, depending on the amount of food and water I was carrying. I had to take it off and put it on many times throughout the day. If I were to lean over to pick up something, I could fall over; if I fell over with it on my back, I was like a turtle on its back wriggling to get up; if I needed to climb straight up a rock, I had to take it off and set it before me or it would drag me down the mountain; if I was thirsty, I had to take it off to get to my water. My pack was my friend as it provided for me, but my enemy when it dragged me down.

I began to think of my pack as the burden of anger. I remembered the verse, "Be ye angry and sin not," (Ephesians 4:26a. King James Version). I knew there was such a thing as righteous anger, but what I was experiencing was sin. It was a burden that I would give up, and then take back again. I began to pray, every time I put my pack on, that it would represent putting on Christ, and not repeatedly carrying a destructive burden. "Come to Me, all you who labor and are heavy laden, and I will give you rest. For My yoke is easy and My burden is light" (Matthew 11:28, 30 New King James Version)

FROM THE JOURNEY   HOT SPRINGS
Tuesday, 5/30/06   270.7 miles north of Springer

The rhododendrons are finally in bloom and boy, are they happy! They blossom all over the trail, sometimes making an arch so I'm totally covered with them. Really pretty. This morning I was the first to break the trail so I got to break the cobwebs. Finally decided to hold one trekking pole out like a torch to open the path. Maybe I looked like Joan of Arc or something. Or something.

Today I'm in town! Hot Springs - Must be 90 degrees. Pavement radiates the heat and I've been sweating buckets. Ate biscuit, cheese and sausage melt, four slices of tomato, hash browns and orange juice at Smokey Mountain Diner. Umph. Followed AT blazes on the side walk over to an outfitter store where they had free internet with limited time, and the library opened at 1pm. I hoped to download pictures from there.

Staying at Elmer's hostel. Wonderful meal, great conversation with Elmer and hikers. Known as The Balladry, it had an old music room where I played a guitar when nobody was listening.

I got a couple of emails. It's weird out here. You get the feeling this is it. This is life. There's nothing else going on. Then reality - oh yeah, other people have lives and they're dealing with real life issues. I pray for others, but somewhat in the dark. But, God knows. Grateful for this time.

Miles hiked on AT today: 3.2

God had my attention on February 20, 1996, when my doctor said the lump on my neck was either cat scratch fever or cancer. He had my attention February 20, 1996, when my daughter called to say her unborn child was a girl with anencephaly. I was told I would live five to fifteen years with Non-Hodgkin's Lymphoma; Christie would die the day she was born.

My faith told me that I could trust God. That this, even this, would work out according to his plan, based upon his love for us. I knew it in my head; I would spend the next several years finding it in my heart.

I received many gifts during that time, but the greatest was an appreciation for time. The preacher said our Christie accomplished more in her brief time than some will in multiple decades of life. Time is really all we have on this earth. Time with God. Time with friends and family. I wrote the following song for my grandchildren:

> "If I were to wish a wish, a wish,
> I wouldn't wish for a dish or fish,
> I wouldn't ask for a mask or flask,
> I'd just want time with you. With who?
> I just want time with you. That's who!"

The mountain path afforded me intimate time with my living, eternal God. "To everything there is a season, a time for every purpose under heaven" (Ecclesiastes 3:1. King James Version)

FROM THE JOURNEY   SPRING MOUNTAIN SHELTER
Wednesday, 5/31/06   281.7 miles north of Springer

My night at camp was uneventful. Ate, unpacked, slept, ate, packed. A routine morning after a routine night in a wooded camp. Nobody around and started my walk and chat with God.

Miles hiked on AT today: 11

FROM THE WELL   A LIGHTED PATH

My time with God was never routine. Sometimes as I hiked I would just focus on one word from a verse to dig out all I knew about it and how it applied to my life. I'd gone miles taking a word from Philippians 4:8, thinking about what it meant. "True." Truth, what is that? Being sure about something? What am I certain about? Paul said, "I know whom I have believed and am persuaded that He is able to keep what I have committed to Him until that Day." (2 Timothy 1:12. New King James Version)

John Muir said, "And into the forest I go to lose my mind and find my soul." Ralph Waldo Emerson described a walk in the woods this way, "In the woods we return to reason and faith."

I came upon a place with light shining down on my path. It warmed my heart. "Thy word is a lamp unto my feet and a light unto my path." (Psalm 119:105 King James Version)

FROM THE JOURNEY   WHITE ROCK CLIFFS
6/1/06   293.4 miles north of Springer

Saw a flag sticking out of a tree. Realized I missed Memorial Day. Used to be May 30th, I guess it's on Mondays now. I spent several miles praying for our country. Can't remember much else that I saw today. Just lots of evidence of God in America. Grateful. "Blessed is the nation whose God is the Lord". (Psalm 33:12 King James Version)

Miles hiked on AT today: 11.7

Our country's motto is, "In God we Trust." What does that mean? Trust for what? Were they just words to guide an infant nation or can God be trusted for more? Can God be trusted personally?

We always had a parade on Memorial Day and I was a proud Girl Scout the year I got to carry the flag. My sister always recited the Gettysburg Address and my brother played "Taps" at the cemetery. So much has changed. So much of throwing out the baby with the bath water. What was so harmful about having the Ten Commandments on our classroom wall?

"If my people, which are called by my name, shall humble themselves, and pray, and seek my face, and turn from their wicked ways; then will I hear from heaven, and will forgive their sin, and will heal their land." (2 Chronicles 7:14 King James Version)

Lord, bless us.

FROM THE JOURNEY   FLINT GAP
6/2/06   302.2 miles north of Springer

Had lunch at a messy shelter today. Entered a limerick in the register.

> There once was a hiker named Slackers,
> In disregard for later backpackers.
> When stopped at a shelter, left trash helter-skelter
> For mice, flies, and other trash-snackers.

Miles hiked on AT today: 9.8

FROM THE WELL   TALKING TRASH

The dump truck came to my house twice weekly and there was usually a full barrel to empty. The same thing happened up and down my street. Why is that? Living in the woods brought new meaning to the term, "Take Out." I was taught as a child camper, "Leave No Trace." Whatever you bring in, take out. What if we had to carry on our backs all the trash we make for a full week until we could drop it into a dumpster? Would we make less trash? Would we be willing to carry somebody else's trash as well?

Some may say, "How silly! Just burn it, throw it, or bury it." Really? Most trash contains plastic, which may give off toxic fumes as it burns. Food thrown into the woods will probably be eaten by animals, and then they are taught that human food is easy to get and yummy to eat even if it is being held by a human hand at the time. Burying might be good, but how deep? Forgot your shovel? Surely an animal won't reach the bacon wrapper I buried with my boot heel.

Planning to accommodate the inevitable trash just makes sense. There will always be trash in our lives, so why do we let it knock us off the path? Why are we surprised by it as though we thought it would never come? There were words of wisdom that I either made up or heard. They brought me through a particularly trashy period of my life and continue to direct me, "You may not always be able to control your circumstances, but you can control your response to them."

FROM THE JOURNEY   BEAUTY SPOT
Monday, 6/3-5/06.   349.5 miles north of Springer

Wet, hungry and anxious because I discovered I had miscalculated the distance between hostels. Lots of hard climbing. Sang praise songs to keep me going. Relieved to catch a ride from a family of day-hikers to Miss Janet's Hostel in Erwin, Tennessee. Had to retrace steps for long way to get the ride but it was worth it. My mail drop box was a welcome site, but my mouth watered for colorful food. She told about a restaurant in town where I could get prime rib, potatoes, bread, salad and desert for ten dollars. I showered, changed into clean clothes and off I went. I couldn't believe it. I could only eat a little salad and a few bites of meat. Was it possible that my stomach could shrink so much? I stayed at the hostel two nights and ate from my leftovers for every meal except for her terrific breakfasts. She had a contest to make an alcohol stove and boil water before another hiker could with his fancy contraption. Miss Janet won. I was able to attend church on Sunday. CVS to develop pictures. Used the internet during the night. Nice to get caught up.

Left Miss Janet's 10-ish. Good walk. The computer screensaver at Miss Janet's was of a beautiful sunset. I asked where the picture was taken and her daughter told me it was a place on the trail called "Beauty Spot." Made it there in the middle of the day so set up tent and took a nap. When I crawled out a few hours later, I saw a man setting up his tripod and camera. It turns out he was a professional published photographer, there to shoot the sunset. "Huh," I thought, "Guess I picked a good spot." Talked for a while. Peaceful sunset, worth the wait.

Miles hiked on AT today: 10.8

FROM THE WELL   SUNSETS

Rare things, sunsets. I had to deliberately stop hiking to find a spot to set up camp so that I might see one. Another precious gift on the trail. "From the rising of the sun to its going down the LORD's name is to be praised." (Psalm 113:3 New King James Version)

FROM THE JOURNEY   CLYDE SMITH SHELTER
Thursday, 6/6/06   363.9 miles north of Springer

Nice sunrise. Loved the walk in morning - Rhodys, Beeches, Firs - really liked the firs and trail with moss, etc. Trees made a maze. Had to watch for the white blazes. Stopped at spring now. Aaron and Ryan went by last night. Met a Thru-hiker, an older lady on her way to Maine, hiking four hours a day. Left in April. Good application of Philippians 4:8 yesterday. Relief. Also - white blazes = Holy Spirit. Comforter.

Camped at Clyde Smith shelter with Wendy, who I met back at Tri-Corner Shelter, Ryan, Aaron and others.

Miles hiked on AT today: 14.4

FROM THE WELL   WHITE BLAZES

A patch of white paint the size and shape of a school eraser. How could such a thing bring such comfort? Yet sometimes I wanted to run up and kiss it. Talk about a tree hugger! The official mark for the Appalachian Trail is a white blaze. Side trails are blue or some other color. But, if you see the white blaze, you know you're on the right trail. Most of the time, you can either see one ahead or one behind.

This was so important to me, particularly at road crossings where there were trails everywhere. Hiking alone, I didn't want to spend any more time than necessary in parking lots and on roads, so I was always relieved to see the blaze. Safety in a white blaze. Comfort from a white blaze.

Before ascending into heaven, Jesus told the disciples he would leave them with a comforter who would guide them and remind them of all the things he had taught them. He gave the same promise to everyone who trusts in him. The white blazes reminded me of that promised Holy Spirit on whom I depended to direct me at life's crossroads. "But the Helper, the Holy Spirit, whom the Father will send in My name, He will teach you all things, and bring to your remembrance all things that I said to you," (John 14:26 New King James Version)

FROM THE JOURNEY   OVERMOUNTAIN SHELTER
06/7/06   376.8 miles north of Springer

Met up with others on top of Roan Mountain. The MOST difficult climb - basically straight uphill from 8:30 am to 1pm. Great view, great day. Then climbed Grassy Ridge - another steep climb but short. Wendy waited for me on top and we hiked together to Over Mountain 12.9 miles in all. The shelter is an old barn overlooking a valley. Really pretty. There's some Revolutionary War history near here about seventy Over Mountain soldiers. I wrote limericks in the register about Wendy, Aaron, Ryan and myself. They thought they were funny. Rainy this am. Thunder and lightening last night. Comfy and dry in here. Wendy and I may hike together to a new shelter at mile 393.9 - that's 17.1 miles away!

Miles hiked on AT today: 12.9

FROM THE WELL   HUMOR

With the title "Joy in the Journey," there ought to be a section on humor. I believe God has a sense of humor, and there was much about my experience on the trail that was funny. The limericks were fun. They came along to fill some long days.

On Wendy conquering Roan Mountain-

    There once was a hiker named Wendy
    Who found that her legs were quite bendy.
    Oh Roan, it was wicked; it's path she has kick-ed,
    And now she can rest, fine, and dandy.

We were hiking with Ryan, and Aaron -

"There once was a hiker named Aaron,
who's friend said, 'Let's hike if you're darin',
He hiked up Roan Mountain,
found fresh water fountain
and now he's grinnin' and bearin'.

There once was a hiker named Ryan,
who marks off the miles without tryin',
He pulls out his maps,
fresh energy he taps,
and last time I saw he was flyin'!

The potential for wild pigs on the trail led me to think about the warthog. Imagine the Father asking the Son, "What shall we do with these spare parts?" He answers, "Let's stick them here and there. Behold! A warthog!" And then they laughed.

Swinging Lick Gap - strange name. No gap. What does swinging lick mean? Mindless for a few mountains - meaning of swing, of lick - getting a licking - bear doing a dance step -

"One foot 'fore the other
Sway from side to side
Ain't no time to take a nap
That's how ya do the swingin' lick gap!"

Hiker to Catterpillar: How far ya goin'?
Catterpillar: Oh, just across this trail.
Hiker: Got that.

Snail to Hiker: "You call yourself a hiker with your two legs, two arms, two poles, huffing and puffing, grunting and groaning? Learn from me. Foot. Mouth. Hat. That's all you need. Good to go."

I was puffing out my last breaths on earth. Done. Finished right there on the trail. Couldn't even finish my limerick;

"There once was a hiker called Pudge.
She moved through the mountains like sludge…"

And there I was. Stuck in sludge. I prayed God to give me the strength to continue when I discovered a turtle. He was right there on the trail, northbound. I didn't know what to say. I mean, what do you say to a turtle that thinks he'll make it to Maine and you're defeated by this little hump after a measly four hundred miles? He just sat there; he didn't even acknowledge my presence. No encouraging words, no offer to carry my pack. Then I thought, "I can do this. I can't do much, but

I can pass this turtle." Stepping over him gave me the burst of energy I needed to finish the day's hike and my limerick:

"She caught up with a turtle, made pole-vaulting hurdle
And hiked on with spring in her trudge!"

While on a forty-day hike, I knew I couldn't be tuned in to God all the time. Yet, regardless of my focus, God had messages for me, sometimes in the most unusual places. I don't know a verse about humor, but I know he means for me to have joy in this journey.

FROM THE JOURNEY   MOUNTAINEER FALLS
6/8/06   393.9 miles north of Springer

Made it to the brand new Mountaineer Falls shelter about 7pm. Big day. Hiked with Wendy. Followed the white blazes through a pasture that belonged to Watusi Longhorns!

Wendy was wearing a red jacket. Run, Wendy, Run! Fun. Lots of tall grass hiking and we got soaked. Great shelter - clean, new, no mice or bears! Made a great dinner of Ramen and Albacore marinated in soy and ginger with her oatmeal, dry fruit and nuts cooked up with brown sugar for dessert.

Miles hiked on AT today: 17.1

FROM THE WELL   TRAIL DAYS

This seems like a good place to describe a typical trail day. Seeing the title, some may have expected a description of Trail Days in Damascus, surprised that I had suddenly turned into a party animal. Sorry to disappoint.

My plan for each day was to walk, eat, drink, and sleep. The next day I might eat, walk, drink, and then sleep. One day, I set up my tent at 2 o'clock for a nap, so that day I ate, walked, slept, drank, walked, ate, and slept again. What may seem pretty sad to some people is that those were some of the best days of my life so far. Doesn't take much to make me happy. I'm reminded of a great line in a favorite hymn, "Trust and Obey," by John H. Sammis: "When we walk with the Lord, in the light of his Word, what a glory he sheds on our way." "This is the day the LORD has made; we will rejoice and be glad in it," (Psalm 118:24 New King James Version)

FROM THE JOURNEY	CAMPSITE
6/9/06	399.3 miles north of Springer

Funny morning - Wendy dreamed we were at this fancy home and just walked in, she made coffee and I made cinnamon toast. Just before we left Mountaineer Shelter I discovered a single packaged Cinnamon Swirl! We laughed, put down our packs, sat at the "table" and cut it in 1/2 with a knife and ate it with finesse. So funny. She made up a limerick about me. It captured my tendency to head in the "wrong" direction.

"There once was a hiker named Sue,
Who never shared a day that was blue,
She'd take off in a swelter, at times helter-skelter,
And preferred her tent to a shelter."

Wendy went on ahead, I wasn't sure I could make it all the way to Kincora.

Miles hiked on AT today: 5.4

FROM THE WELL	CONTENTMENT

Wendy said that was her memory of the first day we met as I approached Tri-Corner Knob Shelter where she was hunkered down. I didn't remember meeting her but she just couldn't believe this weirdo who wasn't bummed by all the rain. I don't know that I never share a day that is blue. I just prefer to count my blessings.

"I know what it is to be in need, and I know what it is to have plenty. I have learned the secret of being content in any and every situation, whether well fed or hungry, whether living in plenty or in want." (Philippians 4:12 New International Version)

FROM THE JOURNEY	DENNIS COVE
6/10/06	409.3 miles north of Springer

Made it to Kincora Hostel (Bob Peoples) - great place. Wendy wanted to go north from Kincora so we split. We had pizza and I found an orange in the fridge. Several people there. Lots of talking - overwhelming. All talking at once. I had to get away.

Miles hiked on AT today: 10

FROM THE WELL	HOSTELS

This section is dedicated to all those trail volunteers, supporters and hostel owners who make it possible for people like me to enjoy the wilderness. The Appalachian Trail Conservancy provided the names of hostels along the trail where I could have my mail drop boxes delivered. I would stay in five welcome retreats as some of my boxes would be sent to post offices.

The first was the unplanned refuge at Neel's Gap in the Walasi-Yi Hostel. Next was Standing Bear Farm in Hartford, TN where I had my own "private" cabin over a stream.

Miss Janet's Hostel in Erwin, Tennessee was a much needed retreat for two night's rest.

Kincora Hostel, run by Bob and Pat Peoples in Hampton, Tennessee, was a highlight. I believe they had trail dirt in their blood stream. I was looking forward to coming back to help with their part of the trail.

I would stay at Mount Rogers Outfitters hostel if I made it to Damascus, prior to meeting friends at Grayson Highlands.

"I thank my God upon every remembrance of you," (Philippians 1:3 New King James Version)

FROM THE JOURNEY   VANDEVENTER SHELTER
Sunday, 6/11/06   426.8 miles north of Springer

Bob suggested a ride to US 321 and hike 8.7 miles south to Kincora then ride back to US 321 and head north. Napsalot and I hiked it together. Pretty falls, saw a snake. I met Wendy at Watauga Shelter. She'd had a tough climb and couldn't go on so I left although she tried to convince me to stay. I pushed on to Vandeventer - scouts there. L-o-n-g uphill along a ridge and thunder all around. I kept praying God to get me there and give me strength. Got there about 6:50 and at scout's insistence, slept in shelter. Scouts tenting all around at the base of rocks and trees. 12:30 am Severe T&L all around and I prayed God's feather over the scouts.

Miles hiked on AT today: 17.3

FROM THE WELL   STORMS

The weather was fairly predictable. In Georgia, I walked through clouds. There was never a view, always mist, dripping trees. I saw my shadow for the first time in North Carolina. Thunderstorms accompanied me through Tennessee. It was rarely a problem. One night I couldn't find enough things to wear or put over me to take away the bitter chill and was saved by lighting my stove in the tent's vestibule and drinking hot lemonade.

Some place in Tennessee I was exposed, for what seemed like hours, on an open ridge. Thunder was clapping, lightning strikes were getting closer, and I had nowhere to go. I was tired and wanted desperately to stop and rest. I admit I was afraid. I was the highest point around and thought about lying where I was until the storm passed. But, the storm looked big like it was there to stay. I knew there was a shelter ahead and I needed to get to safety.

In the hymn "How Great Thou Art," the author Carl Boberg said, "I hear the rolling thunder… and then proclaim, 'My God! How great thou art!' " I thought, "If he could praise God in the storm, so could I."

I recalled years earlier being caught in a storm. Stretched out on the floor of my tent while what turned out to be a tornado passed through, I had made up a song. I sang it then as I walked, "Jesus calmed the storm, he'll calm the storm in me."

"He calms the storm, so that its waves are still," (Psalm 107: 29 New King James Version)

FROM THE JOURNEY   DOUBLE SPRINGS SHELTER
Monday, 6/12/06   441.2 miles north of Springer

Made it to Double Springs - more scouts #39 from Burlington, NC. They were sleeping in the shelter so I hung with them at campsite until 8 or so and set up tent at campsite - T&L and hard rain throughout night but misty in am, out at 8:30 .

Miles hiked on AT today: 14.4

FROM THE WELL   SOLO HIKING

From its very conception, this was to be a solo hike. I was a new divorcee when I started planning and many acquaintances suggested it might be a good place to find a man. There were some who wanted to join me, possibly to become that man. I wasn't interested. I was in pretty good shape emotionally and thanks to a quotation I had memorized early in my single life, I was feeling pretty strong spiritually. I found it online while looking for God's perspective on the single life. About abiding in God alone, Luci Swindoll wrote, "Assuming the single person is a believer, the answer to companionship is learning to obey God. We must have a real, working relationship with the Lord. When we know him as a person, as a companion, then trust, obedience, contentment and service are fruits of that relationship." My hike was a consequence of my beliefs.

When people expressed concern about hiking alone, I tried to make them understand that I would not be alone because God was going with me. I was totally and completely sure of this. It never once occurred to me that I was or would be alone. The fact that I would not be hiking with people was deliberate; I did not want them to crowd God out of my hike. I knew that he would bring things to mind. I knew that he would suggest people to pray for. I knew that he wanted to carry some of my heavy stuff. Other people would have distracted me.

I'm not saying I never walked with anybody else. I would have been robbed of an important part of the trail experience. The trail community was precious, but my time alone with God was my most cherished. I still find my closest time of companionship with God is when I am walking, be it in my neighborhood, at the beach, or down a wooded path. "He has shown you, O man, what is good; And what does the LORD require of you but to do justly, to love mercy, and to walk humbly with your God?" (Micah 6:8 New King James Version)

VIRGINIA

FROM THE JOURNEY
Tuesday, 6/13/06

DAMASCUS
459.5 miles north of Springer

Hiked 18.3 miles today, my biggest day. Celebrated as I stepped over the line from Tennessee to Virginia! Pushed on with my first, and only, blister and made it to Mount Rogers Outfitters(MRO)/ Dave's Place where I met several hikers enjoying "0" days. I'd met them back at Icewater Shelter. Others always made it to places before me. Maybe it's that they hiked faster, or maybe they just maintained a northerly direction. Showered, laundered, ate supper of yucky hamburger but yummy OJ/Cranberry/Sprite/Vanilla ice cream soda.

Can't believe I'm here. A few more days of hiking and then some trail maintenance back in Tennessee and I will have spent forty days on the Appalachian Trail. I'm blown away.

Miles hiked on AT today: 18.3

FROM THE WELL

SUFFICIENCY

As I reflect, I wonder how this trip happened. I had never prepared for anything ahead of time in my life. My middle name was "Procrastination." I never did today what could be put off until tomorrow. In school, all my papers were written sometime after midnight on their due date. In college I studied in the parking lot prior to sitting for my exams. Who was this person? All I can say is that this was to be God's hike. I had committed it to the One who has an eternity of time yet wastes none. One with infinite resources yet provides according to need. I did what I could but leaned on him for everything. The result? I earned one tiny blister on my second right toe after pushing eighteen miles one day in wet socks. I had a cold sore for a few days. The rest? All good.

"Therefore I say to you, do not worry about your life, what you will eat or what you will drink; nor about your body, what you will put on. Is not life more than food and the body more than clothing? Look at the birds of the air, for they neither sow nor reap nor gather into barns; yet your heavenly Father feeds them. Are you not more valuable than they?" (Matthew 6:25-26 New King James Version)

FROM THE JOURNEY   GRAYSON HIGHLANDS/Wise Shelter
6/14/06 Wednesday   492.6 miles north of Springer

3:30 pm Wow. Am I actually here? Had trouble sleeping at Dave's Place due to some kind of intermittent compressor noise. Got up and went to Sunday Outfitters to see about downloading pictures after breakfast of biscuit and gravy at Exxon. Got that done and back down to MRO about 10:30. Found out $50 for shuttle to Grayson Highlands (GH) which wasn't available anyway. They said it would take all day to hitch a ride to GH and I would need to walk about two miles out of town first. Yuck. I packed up and headed out. Asked at MRO and gas station then walked the marked trail through town until I came to Old Barn Rental — "Sure, hop in that van" $5. Then they called me back to hop in Jeep with power company guy who was going directly to GH. Awesome. He dropped me off at 12:30.

Grayson Highlands National Park. Am I really here?

I looked at a map and started walking asphalt toward Massie Gap. Maintenance guy offered ride, hiked A-spur/Rhododendron Trail to AT North, hiked to Wise Shelter for last register entry. Took Horse Trail down to campground, and fell into hugs with Pat then Jan. Can't describe the emotions I was feeling. Camped right across from Bluegrass guys — they played until about 11pm. Really good. Nice campfire. Dinner of Alfredo with chicken, brownie and cupcakes. FTA campers came over and enjoyed my pictures. Rachael was a real help identifying the flowers. Looking forward to exploring the trails around here. This may have been my final destination, but I don't want to be done. So much meaning in that saying, "It's the journey, not the destination."

Miles of AT skipped: 30.3
Miles hiked on AT today: 2.8+

FROM THE WELL   WISE SHELTER REGISTER ENTRY

Written in the register: "Got a ride from Damascus to Massie Gap to hike here for what will be my last Register entry. Finishing up my forty-day GA-VA Journey. Will slack-pack with friends for a couple more days. Driving up to Georgia in May, I saw the mountains with great anticipation and thought up this song: "Hey Mountain, what's your name? Have you secrets, what's your game? Will you leave me whole or lame? Hey Mountain, what's your name?" I'll admit, I still don't know their names but I leave them whole-er than whole. I came wanting to experience God in a deeper way, in his creation. I got that, and more. The people, the sights, the sounds - the whole adventure has been awesome. To all you hikers who continue may you seek and find peace and joy in your individual journeys.

Two scripture verses have carried me: Philippians 4:8 which is about our thoughts and Psalm 91, the Hiker's Psalm with the promise that we'll be covered with God's feathers for protection.

Happy Thoughts + Happy Talk = Happy Walk
"Happy Talk"
Joy in the Journey

P.S. Wish Wendy a Happy Birthday 6/26!"

FROM THE JOURNEY   GRAYSON HIGHLANDS/Thomas Knob
6/15/06, Thursday   489.8 miles north of Springer

Slept fair in tent at the campground — missed the trail and aware of others around. Up about 7 - Peanut butter and bread, cheese and apple for breakfast with coffee.

Rode the Virginia Creeper Trail with FTA from White Top Station to Damascus. Stopped at Green Cove Station where I bought Jerry Greer's post cards, the photographer from Beauty Spot. Cool. Awesome ride, met a few AT hikers including the veteran with an artificial leg who is on the third hike of the Triple Crown having completed the Pacific Crest of 2,654 miles, the Continental Divide of 3,100 miles and now the Appalachian Trail. Hope he makes it to Katahdin to total about 7,900 miles. Amazing.

Hiked Rhododendron Trail to AT south to Rhododendron Gap with some FTA members. Played with feral ponies! I continued on 0.8 mi south to Thomas Knob shelter and saw from the register that Needles, Fire and Ice and Wendy had been there. I met a couple and started chatting about the trail, and then I asked their trail names. I was never so surprised to discover they were the very ones who had carried me four hundred miles; yet we were just meeting for the first time, BlueFeather and Daisy - cool. Christians. Met two lady SOBO's on five-day sectional hikes, and they said they'd been to Wise last night and F&I and Wendy had been there too. Said they knew me from register entries. Cool. Group dinner tonight. Talked with one of the FTA group who thru-hiked in '04.

Miles hiked on AT today: 2.3, Miles biked on AT today: 5

FROM THE WELL   WORDS

I always looked forward to the register entries of two hikers in particular named Blue Feather and Daisy. I had not met them but I had known them since Georgia. They never said they were Christians but their entries were always inspiring. It occurred to me that God's Word is like a shelter register, letters written to encourage and guide us along life's journey.

As I made my final entry in the register at Wise Shelter in Grayson Highlands, words were hard to choose. Who would read them? What would they think? Some had thanked me for scriptures I had entered, but no doubt some thought it a misuse of the register. In defense, I never tried to force my hike on anybody. But wait…this wasn't my hike.

FROM THE JOURNEY   GRAYSON HIGHLANDS/The Scales
6/16/06, Friday   495.4 miles north of springer

Hiked to The Scales, the most northern point of my journey. There was a corral with horses and riders preparing for their own AT adventure. I gazed north at the post bearing the white blaze and longed for more.

I saw a T-shirt someplace that said, "Sunday, Monday, Tuesday, Wednesday, Thursday, Friday, Saturday…see? No Someday."

Miles hiked on AT today 3.5

FROM THE WELL   DUPLICATION

Some will no-doubt ask if I will come back, maybe finish The Trail. While the actual hiking part of this journey has been awesome and I would love to see what's over that hill, around that corner, beyond those trees, I know this journey will never be duplicated. It will join the other events in my life that I will always cherish but not repeat. This well is full.

FROM THE JOURNEY   TRAIL MAINTENANCE
Tuesday, 6/20/06   Green Cove, TN

Got a ride from Grayson Highlands to my car in Boone, NC. Took a while to figure out how to drive, to move forward without watching my feet.

When I returned to do some trail maintenance at Kincora after my hike, there were several women authors there who Bob was shuttling around. I didn't get to talk with them, but I just knew somehow the story of the trail needed to be written at least one more time.

Staying at Kincora to pay back - vacuumed the bunk room and took all the mattress covers to wash and dry at the laundry. Doing some trail maintenance by weed-whacking a section of tall grass, my last steps on the beloved trail.

CONCLUSION

FROM THE WELL   JOY IN YOUR JOURNEY

God had joined me on this path. We had shared forty days, and I received all the blessings. I found that the mountains had left me whole, not lame, and I came away with greater assurance of God's involvement in the most minute details of my life. I was leaving the trail with trust in the path he had chosen for me, secure in his protection, satisfied with his provision. And what did he ask in return? Here it is. "These things I have spoken to you, that my joy may remain in you, and that your joy may be full," (John 15:11 New King James Version)

I pray this book has helped you discover some of that joy.

Happy Thoughts + Happy Talk = Happy Walk
Joy in Your Journeys Phil 4:8,9
Happy Talk GA-VA '06

ACKNOWLEDGMENTS

Two years after my hike I received another gift, my husband, Larry Conley, who has been awesome in his patience and support while this book consumed me. I'll make dinner any day now.

The experience could not have happened without the volunteers, Eagle scouts and organizations who make the Trail possible to traverse for people like me. Their handiwork on the trail was evident in abundance.

This book was fourteen years in the making. There were many who would persist in asking when I would write my book and insisted it was a story that needed to be told. I am grateful for their encouragement

Finally, I write with gratitude to those pushy Westbow people who finally stopped accepting my answer that I was not ready to write, and to my friend Barbara Hanson Benedict who showed up at just the right time to help with the conveyance of my thoughts to written words.

ABOUT THE AUTHOR

Sue Hatch, aka "Happy Talk" is an old grandma who never carried a backpack or slept in the woods alone. Her family thought she'd lost her mind. But she requested time off from her very sane job as a visiting nurse and embarked on a walk in the woods that would take her from Georgia to Virginia. Why? To experience the Emmanuel God who really is with us, and means to bring us joy.

Printed in the United States
By Bookmasters